Library as Place:
Rethinking Roles,
Rethinking Space

Council on Library and Information Resources

Washington, D.C.

February 2005

JUL - - 2005

ISBN 1-932326-13-8
ISBN 978-1-932326-13-0
CLIR Publication No. 129

Published by:

Council on Library and Information Resources
1755 Massachusetts Avenue, NW, Suite 500
Washington, DC 20036
Web site at http://www.clir.org

Contents

About the Authors

Scott Bennett is Yale University librarian emeritus. He has had extensive experience with library planning, construction, renovation, and restoration at Yale and in his service as the Sheridan Director of the Milton S. Eisenhower Library at Johns Hopkins University and as assistant university librarian for collection management at Northwestern University. As one of the founders of Project Muse, he fostered changes in information use that drive innovations in the use of library spaces. Bennett has served on both the library and the English department faculties of the University of Illinois at Urbana-Champaign. He is the author of the recent CLIR publication *Libraries Designed for Learning*. He is senior adviser for the Library Project of the Council of Independent Colleges.

Sam Demas is college librarian and senior lecturer at Carleton College. He and his staff are experimenting with the development of the liberal arts college library as both a virtual space and a vibrant place of student research, community building, and cultural events. He and his colleagues are working to define the role of the library in a residential learning community. Before coming to Carleton in 1998, Demas worked at Cornell University for 20 years in a variety of positions and libraries, including head of collection development and preservation at the A. R. Mann Library and associate director of Mann Library. His research interests at Cornell were selection for preservation, national preservation planning, and adapting the principles and practices of collection development to the electronic library.

Geoffrey T. Freeman, AIA, is a principal of Shepley Bulfinch Richardson and Abbott, a Boston-based design firm. A nationally recognized authority on library planning and design, Freeman has designed more than 80 libraries. His chief interest is in contributing to the advancement of education, to understanding how people learn, and to heightened appreciation of how architecture affects the teaching and learning processes. Freeman has taught at the secondary school level and was an instructor in the Department of Visual and Environmental Studies at Harvard College while earning his master of architecture and master in landscape architecture degrees from the Harvard University Graduate School of Design. His clients include Colby College, Brown University, Bucknell University, Emory University, the University of Southern California, Princeton University, Illinois Wesleyan University, Columbia University, Dartmouth College, Lake Forest College, Harvard University, Yale University, Rice University, and Duke University. He frequently lectures about the design of libraries for research universities and liberal arts colleges.

Bernard Frischer is director of the Institute for Advanced Technology in the Humanities, University of Virginia. From 1976 to 2004 he was professor of classics at the University of California, Los Angeles (UCLA), where he founded and directed the Cultural Virtual Reality Laboratory, chaired his department, and was director of the UCLA office of the Education Abroad Program of the University of California. In addition to his work in digital archaeology, he has been involved in fieldwork and excavation, serving as director of the Horace's Villa Project of the American Academy in Rome (1996 to 2003) and of the Frontale di Borgorose Project (2004 to the present). Frischer earned his BA in classics from Wesleyan University and his PhD in classical philology from the University of Heidelberg. He has won many fellowships and awards, including a Michigan Junior Fellowship, the Rome Prize Fellowship in Classics from the American Academy in Rome, two Senior Fellowships from the American Council of Learned Societies, and a Senior Fellowship at the Center for Advanced Studies in the Visual Arts at the National Gallery in Washington, D.C. He is the author of four books and many articles.

Kathleen Burr Oliver, MSLS, MPH, is associate director of the Welch Library and responsible for the library's communication and liaison programs. She also serves as a faculty member in the Johns Hopkins Division of Health Sciences Informatics. Before coming to Hopkins in 1998, Oliver managed a number of small scientific and medical libraries, including those of National Institute of Allergy and Infectious Diseases' Rocky Mountain Laboratory, the American College of Cardiology, and American Medical Association's Washington, D.C., office. She was a reference librarian and search analyst at the National Institutes of Health library, the library of the Pharmaceutical Manufacturers' Association, and UCLA's Biomedical Library. She was project director for a literature review on the cost of illness that was conducted by Georgetown University's Public Services Laboratory, and, with funding from the National Science Foundation, developed Web resources on science topics for the public radio documentary group Soundprint. Her public health training focused on maternal and child health policy, planning, and evaluation. She holds an undergraduate degree in biology and chemistry.

Christina A. Peterson is a librarian in the Academic Services Department of the Dr. Martin Luther King Jr. Library in San José, California. Her responsibilities include coordinating distance-library services, serving as a liaison to departments in the health professions and social sciences, and delivering library outreach to faculty. During the planning process for the King Library, she co-led the User Services Team which developed all public services including reference, circulation, and the new library's Web site. She received her BS in Natural Resources from Humboldt State University in California and her MSLIS from the Catholic University in Washington D.C.

Preface

We are still far from the day when students, researchers, and teachers can access entire research collections from their desktops. Nonetheless, a wealth of high-quality material is now accessible electronically. What does this revolutionary change mean for the creation and design of library space? What is the role of a library when it no longer needs to be a warehouse of books and when users can obtain information without setting foot in its doors? Few libraries have failed to consider these questions—whether they serve their collections electronically or physically, whether they serve the general public or more specialized academic users.

In developing this publication, CLIR sought to explore these questions from a variety of perspectives. Authors of these essays include librarians, an architect, and a professor of art history and classics. The focus is primarily on research and academic libraries, although one essay, in describing a unique merger, challenges the boundaries that have long divided academic and public libraries. Each author brings a distinctive perspective to thinking about the use and services, and the roles and future, of the library; at the same time, each underscores the central, growing importance of the library as *place*—or base—for teaching, learning, and research in the digital age.

The publication is intended to stimulate thinking about the role of the library in the digital age, about the potential—and the imperative—for libraries to meet new needs, and about how these needs will influence the design of physical space. It is written for librarians and others involved in library planning as well as for those who invest in libraries, such as provosts, presidents, and business officers. Its goal is not to catalog all the innovation occurring in libraries nationwide but rather to expose an array of perspectives on the future of the library and to describe how these visions are being manifest in spatial design. We hope that the essays will be useful as a foundation for discussion, questions, and new thinking.

Kathlin Smith
Director of Communications

The Library as Place:

Changes in Learning Patterns, Collections, Technology, and Use

Geoffrey T. Freeman, AIA

Since the rise of universities across Europe during the Age of Enlightenment, the academic library has always held a central position as the heart of an institution—both symbolically and in terms of its physical placement. Preeminently sited and often heroic in scale and character, the library has served as a visual anchor for the surrounding buildings on campus. These early academic libraries were very different from those of the monastic tradition from which they emerged. Unlike the medieval cloistered buildings that were frequented only by monks, libraries at such venerable institutions as Cambridge University and Trinity College at the University of Dublin were both centers of learning and important gathering places for scholars throughout the Western world. Richly embellished with stained glass windows, paneled with ornately carved oak, and appointed with marble statuary commemorating Greek and Roman philosophers, these libraries exuded an almost palpable sense of spiritual and intellectual contemplation. As a "temple of scholarship," the library as place assumed an almost sanctified role, reflected both in its architecture and in its siting.

As developed for more than 200 years, academic libraries in the United States and abroad have generally been designed first and foremost as places to collect, access, and preserve print collections. To enter and use them was considered a privilege. Despite their handsome exteriors, the interior spaces were often dim and confining, the buildings were difficult to navigate, and specialized services and collections were inaccessible to all but the serious scholar. Libraries were revered but, with the exception of providing expanding collections, were comparatively static buildings. Planning and design of these facilities were primarily devoted to the preservation and security of materials and to the efficiency of the library collection services. Prime space was routinely reserved for processing materials.

Given this longstanding practice, it is no surprise that the traditional library we inherit today is not the library of the future. To meet today's academic needs as well as those in the future, the library must reflect the values, mission, and goals of the institution of which it is a part, while also accommodating myriad new information and learning technologies and the ways we access and use them. As an extension of the classroom, library space needs to embody new pedagogies, including collaborative and interactive learning modalities. Significantly, the library must serve as the principal building on campus where one can truly experience and benefit from the centrality of an institution's intellectual community.

Reinventing the Library—Technology as Catalyst

With the emergence and integration of information technology, many predicted that the library would become obsolete. Once students had the option of using their computers anywhere on campus—in their residence halls, at the local cyber café, or under a shady tree in the quad—why would they need to go to the library? Those charged with guiding the future of a college or university demanded that this question be answered before they committed any additional funding to perpetuate the "library"—a facility that many decision makers often considered little more than a warehouse for an outmoded medium for communication or scholarship. Many asserted that the virtual library would replace the physical library. The library as a place would no longer be a critical component of an academic institution.

While information technology has not replaced print media, and is not expected to do so in the foreseeable future, it has nonetheless had an astonishing and quite unanticipated impact on the role of the library. Contrary to the predictions of diminishing use and eventual obsolescence of libraries, usage has expanded dramatically—sometimes doubling or even tripling. These increases are particularly common at libraries and institutions that have worked with their architects and planners to anticipate the full impact of the integration of new information technologies throughout their facilities. At institutions where such collaborative planning has occurred—for our firm, at the University of Southern California, Emory University, and Dartmouth College, and more recently, at Fordham University, Illinois Wesleyan University, and Lake Forest College—new library usage speaks for itself: The demand for services and technological access to information, regardless of format, is beyond expectations.

The library, which is still a combination of the past (print collections) and the present (new information technologies), must be viewed with a new perspective and understanding if it is to fulfill its potential in adding value to the advancement of the institution's academic mission and in moving with that institution into the future. Rather than threatening the traditional concept of the library, the integration of new information technology has actually become the catalyst that transforms the library into a more vital and critical intellectual center of life at colleges and universities today.

The library is the only centralized location where new and emerging information technologies can be combined with traditional knowledge resources in a user-focused, service-rich environment that supports today's social and educational patterns of learning, teaching, and research.

When beginning to conceptualize and plan a library for the future, we must first ask an obvious question: If faculty, scholars, and students can now obtain information in any format and access it anywhere on campus, then why does the library, as a physical place, play such an important role in the renewal and advancement of an institution's intellectual life? The answer is straightforward: The library is the only centralized location where new and emerging information technologies can be combined with traditional knowledge resources in a user-focused, service-rich environment that supports today's social and educational patterns of learning, teaching, and research. Whereas the Internet has tended to isolate people, the library, as a physical place, has done just the opposite. Within the institution, as a reinvigorated, dynamic learning resource, the library can once again become the centerpiece for establishing the intellectual community and scholarly enterprise.

When Shepley Bulfinch Richardson and Abbott prepared the programmatic concept for the renovation and expansion of the Perkins Library at Duke University, we asked a student why he used the library. He replied that when he "got serious," that was the only place he wanted to be. This attitude is surprisingly consistent wherever we have recently renovated or added to library facilities. Students at all levels of academic proficiency need and want to go to the library now more than ever before. Going to the library adds value to their lives and offers many of the tools and experiences that will give them the competitive edge they will need to succeed after their formal education is completed. There is an expectation that the library is the place to be; it is where the action is.

People often ask, "What recently completed library can I visit that exemplifies the perfect library design?" Consistently, and regretfully, we reply that no single, ideal example exists. When undertaking a new project, it is important to analyze a wide variety of successful planning and design elements from as many projects as possible. Our objective is to draw from the best of these elements and to add to them in new ways to meet the unique requirements of a given institution's library program today and the future.

As we go forward, we must recognize the meaningful contribution that the library can provide *if* planned correctly. The goal of effective planning is to make the experience and services of the library transparent to the user. Rather than hide resources, the library should bring them to the user, creating a one-stop shopping experience. Whether users access e-mail, digitized resources, or special print collections, or are reformatting and publishing a paper, the library should be the place to enable them to advance their learning experiences.

The Berry-Baker Library at Dartmouth is an excellent example of a facility where a newly renovated and expanded library space, combined with computing and interactive media functions, was planned with how students learn and communicate in this new information age foremost in mind. In the planning stage, we asked several questions that included: Why do students enter the library? What is the sequence of use of the services or technology students require? How should service points be configured with respect to anticipated types of inquiry and use patterns? Do we bring together library staff in a central information commons, or should they remain with specific collections or services? What configuration of services is most flexible?

The resolution of these issues generated the formation of the library as a unique place. Although the Dartmouth library has been designed around a carefully thought-out service and activity pattern, its real test will be over time in terms of the ability of its central information space to adapt to evolving patterns of use without losing the order and transparency of its basic organizational idea.

Libraries as Learning Laboratories

As new technologies are created that increasingly inform the learning experience, any institution seriously considering the future of its libraries must reach a consensus on the role that it wants these facilities to play in meeting the needs not only of its current academic community but also of the community it aspires to create in the future. The principal challenge for the architect is to design a learning and research environment that is transparent and sufficiently flexible to support this evolution in use. However, we must not design space that is so generic or anonymous that it lacks the distinctive quality that should be expected for such an important building. The charge to architects is to create libraries that, themselves, *learn.* One key concept is that the library as a place must be self-organizing—that is, sufficiently flexible to meet changing space needs. To accomplish this, library planners must be more entrepreneurial in outlook, periodically evaluating the effective use of space and assessing new placements of services and configurations of learning spaces in response to changes in user demand.

At recent master-planning projects for the libraries at Massachusetts Institute of Technology and Rice University, each institution developed a vision for their facilities based on a thorough analysis of how and when students did their academic work. At both universities, they found that this was primarily between 11:00 p.m. and 4:00 a.m.—the very period when libraries are typically closed. Planning for libraries today should be premised on 24-hour access, with critical services and technology provided and located when and where they are needed.

The use of electronic databases, digitized formats, and interactive media has also fostered a major shift from the dominance of independent study to more collaborative and interactive learning. A student can go to this place called the "library" and see it as a logical extension of the classroom. It is a place to access and explore with fellow students information in a variety of formats, analyze the information in group discussion, and produce a publication or a presentation for the next day's seminar.

To address this need, libraries must provide numerous technology-infused group study rooms and project-development spaces. As "laboratories that learn," these spaces are designed to be easily reconfigured in response to new technologies and pedagogies. In this interactive learning environment, it is important to accommodate the sound of learning—lively group discussions or intense conversations over coffee—while controlling the impact of acoustics on surrounding space. We must never lose sight of the dedicated, contemplative spaces that will remain an important aspect of any place of scholarship.

Ten or fifteen years ago, we were taking all the teaching facilities out of libraries. The goal was to "purify" the library—to separate it from the classroom experience. Today, these spaces are not only back in the library, but in a more dynamic way than ever. Although they sometimes add to the stock of the institution's teaching spaces, more significantly, they take advantage of a potential to become infused with new information technologies in a service-rich environment.

Now . . . faculty expect their students to use their time in the library thinking analytically, rather than simply searching for information.

In this regard, the faculty plays a significant role in drawing students to the library. Now that information is available almost instantaneously anywhere on campus, faculty expect their students to use their time in the library thinking analytically, rather than simply searching for information. Faculty also see the library as an extension of the classroom, as a place in which students engage in a collaborative learning process, a place where they will, it is hoped, develop or refine their critical thinking.

Several years ago, we designed a number of facilities in academic libraries that were expressly aimed at helping faculty members advance their own understanding and use of changing information technologies. As faculty members have become increasingly sophisticated in their use of technology, we now provide special kinds of teaching spaces for the application of these skills. At the same time, traditional and often-arbitrary boundaries among disciplines are breaking down. In response to these changes, interactive presentation spaces and virtual reality labs are becoming the norm. Faculty members can now make connections with interrelated disciplines or disciplines other than their own and access resources, regardless of their locations. The library is regarded as the laboratory for the humanist and social scientist.

When we were planning to renovate the Countway Library at Harvard Medical School, a senior researcher gave us a clue as to how the library was being used in this new information age. He stated that as a result of electronic access to information, the pace of his research had increased exponentially. What used to take two weeks could now be completed in two hours. As a result of this efficiency, the researcher's postdoctoral fellows were asked to be in the library on a regular basis and charged with evaluating resources and acquiring publications at a pace never before imagined—a research method that became known as "search and seize." This time-sensitive pattern of use not only provided our planning team with an understanding of how the library continues to be a critical part of the intellectual life of an institution but also gave us insight into how to organize various functions to most efficiently serve its users. Understanding the horizontal and vertical relationship of services and collections was paramount to our discussions.

A Place for Community, Contemplation

One of the fascinating things that we are now observing is the impact of redesigned library space on the so-called "psychosocial" aspects of an academic community. The library's primary role is to advance and enrich the student's educational experience; however, by cutting across all disciplines and functions, the library also serves a significant social role. It is a place where people come together on levels and in ways that they might not in the residence hall, classroom, or off-campus location. Upon entering the library, the student becomes part of a larger community—a community that endows one with a greater sense of self and higher purpose. Students inform us that they want their library to "feel bigger than they are." They want to be part of the richness of the tradition of scholarship as well as its expectation of the future. They want to experience a sense of inspiration.

While students are intensely engaged in using new technologies, they also want to enjoy the library as a contemplative oasis. Interestingly, a significant majority of students still considers the traditional reading room their favorite area of the library—the great, vaulted, light-filled space, whose walls are lined with books they may never pull off the shelf.

The Planning Process

The way in which we plan libraries today has changed significantly. Planners and designers define space in response to anticipated user patterns, identifying the physical characteristics of this space and the specific value it will add to the educational mission of the institution as a whole. Previously, program requirements were developed in response to carefully defined comparative library standards, such as the number of books to be housed, the number of seats for a particular style of study, or the number of square feet required for a specific technical support function. The quick and easy solution to any perceived need was formula driven—always to add more space.

Very often, this was the wrong response. Too much space has already been built in the name of library "needs" without any real understanding of the true value or contribution of expanded or renovated facilities to the institution's long-term future. The library today must function foremost as an integral and interdependent part of the institution's total educational experience.

Achieving this goal requires a collaborative planning process. That process must include the library director, members of the administration, trustees, students, and faculty, and it must begin *before* a program for space needs is developed. Questions that should be addressed include the following: How should the "library," and its

Designing a library that functions as an integral and interdependent part of the institution's total educational experience requires collaborative planning that includes the library director, members of the administration, trustees, students, and faculty.

services and its collections, serve the institution? What programs not in the library at present should be in the facility in the future? How does the library add value to the academic experience of the students and faculty? How is the library presently perceived, and how can it function as an interdependent facility with other learning and teaching opportunities on a campus in the future? How much of the traditional library program must remain in a centralized facility? How does the library reflect the vision of the institution of which it is part?

It is our belief that library facilities are most successful when they are conceived to be an integral part of the institution as a whole. It is no longer acceptable to consider libraries as stand-alone facilities. In the conceptual program phase of a facility, consideration must be given not only to anticipated learning patterns but also to the goals and the culture of the institution. We must consider the type of student and faculty an institution wants to attract and retain; the library plays a critical role in this respect. Once we understand the potential of the library, its role, and the value it adds to the educational experience, we can develop a detailed program to explore alternatives for spatial organization as a means to fulfill an educational vision. Only then can we create a unique physical response to the needs and aspirations of a given institution.

With this in mind, the architect and the institution need to develop a partnership, sharing a vision and goals. It has often been said that an architect cannot create a great library without a great client. A look at the planning-process model for some of our recent projects illustrates this principle.

When Duke University and Dartmouth College began to discuss "expanding" their libraries, each created a library task force and charged it with developing a vision for the library within the context of the institution. Representing the outcome of a meaningful discussion between faculty, students, library professionals, and university administrators, each group's vision became the basis for the multi-year, planning and design effort to follow. These were exemplary efforts.

An initial challenge for any design team is to create physical space that is program driven, yet not so specific to the institution of today that it will not be viable in the future. Working with many clients on similar projects enables us to balance present demands and unidentified future goals and needs. Each time we begin work with an institution, we are able to ask more-informed questions; we have become very good listeners.

Early program and planning decisions have a major impact on the budget, the quality of work, potential interruptions to ongoing services, and ongoing operations and maintenance. Intensive dialogue helps the client's planning and decision-making team understand the physical implications of its planning goals. Institutions today are asking for and receiving much greater accountability for the use of their library space. They need to know how it enhances the institution's educational mission and at what cost.

Once a project is completed, we have had the opportunity to

learn from the staff and users how specific spaces, organizational ideas, or design details have performed. It is through an analysis of the successes and disappointments of planning decisions and architectural expressions on previous projects that the architect begins to understand how to approach future opportunities. It is a never-ending cycle; elements of the past are critically evaluated and lessons are learned.

Flexibility for the Future

If libraries are to remain dynamic, the spaces that define them and the services they offer must continually stimulate users to create new ways of searching and synthesizing materials. There is no question that almost all the library functions being planned for today will need to be reconfigured in the not-too-distant future. While certain principal design elements—such as the articulation of the perimeter wall, the introduction and control of natural light, and the placement of core areas for stairs, toilets, and heating, ventilation, and air conditioning—will remain relatively constant, the majority of space must be capable of adapting to changes in use. If this is to happen, a number of fundamental considerations must be addressed.

Institutions today are asking for and receiving much greater accountability for the use of their library space. They need to know how it enhances the institution's educational mission and at what cost.

In the past, expanding collections reduced user space; now, it is just the opposite. Technology has enriched user space, and the services for its support are increasing at a much faster pace than ever anticipated. Today, we are asked to consider whether a facility can accommodate dense, compact shelving or whether collections should be moved off site. Is the library to be a major research facility, responsible for the acquisition and preservation of substantial collections, or, like the recently completed Lake Forest College library, is the library to focus its energy and space on teaching and learning? Regardless of any specific answer, one thing is common to all: If an institution's goal is to increase and celebrate scholarly activity on its campus, then a flexible, reinvigorated library must become a focus of its community.

Designing the Leavey Library at the University of Southern California a number of years ago provided us with our first opportunity to combine academic computing, media, and reference services into a single, user environment. Based upon intense dialogue and the identified need for a new type of teaching/learning facility, a vision was developed for a so-called "gateway library" to house a relatively new concept at the time—a library focused around a central information commons. At the same time, an equally important design element was the definition of "laboratory space" where faculty members would come to create new curricula and learning models through partnerships with leaders in the publishing and information management industry. Despite careful planning to define specific space requirements for the collaborative research functions identified by the users, technology evolved much more quickly than could be anticipated, and what we thought to be cutting-edge spaces were out of date within the year. The demand was beyond any expectation. We learned that space for the learning and research of tomorrow must be generically conceived and delivered, using construction techniques and infrastructures in imaginative ways that are readily adaptable to reconfiguration.

In trying to anticipate the challenges that the academic library must face if it is to remain vital in the future, the Dartmouth College Library task force charged our design team with the following mandate: all program design elements within the building should, if possible, be planned to accommodate change. Designed in association with Venturi Scott Brown and Associates in Philadelphia, our challenge was to determine how to combine and locate evolving user service points while respecting the unique configuration and quality of public space. The goal was to create a seamless flow of intellectual inquiry and exploration throughout the facility.

Large, open spaces were designed to be reconstructable, so that they could be reconfigured to meet future needs. Enclosed areas for conference rooms, private and semiprivate offices, seminar rooms, and group study rooms were planned so that in the future, these spaces could be incorporated into the open reference and computing commons area. Future needs at Dartmouth will be met by continuing to reconfigure space within the library building itself, not by future expansion. Given these challenges, we must constantly explore and reinvent the concept of flexibility but do so in space of a quality that offers a distinctive, intellectually rich environment for learning, teaching, and research.

Conclusion

The academic library as place holds a unique position on campus. No other building can so symbolically and physically represent the academic heart of an institution. If the library is to remain a dynamic life force, however, it must support the academic community in several new ways. Its space must flexibly accommodate evolving information technologies and their usage as well as become a "laboratory" for new ways of teaching and learning in a wired or wireless environment. At the same time, the library, by its architectural expression and siting, must continue to reflect the unique legacy and traditions of the institution of which it is part. It must include flexible spaces that "learn" as well as traditional reading rooms that inspire scholarship. By embracing these distinct functions, the library as a place can enhance the excitement and adventure of the academic experience, foster a sense of community, and advance the institution into the future. The library of the future remains irreplaceable.

Righting the Balance

Scott Bennett

Making a Paradigm Shift

Over the last decade, colleges and universities in the United States have invested almost a half-billion dollars every year in new and renovated academic libraries. At that level of investment and with the long life cycles demanded of library buildings, we need to know what we are doing. While there is much to celebrate in recent library architecture and few stories of design failure, we nonetheless confront a sobering uncertainty. Architect Craig Hartman describes it as follows:

> Because libraries today are in transition, both as institutions and as a building type, every library that embarks on a building program is in a sense on its own. While there is a long tradition to draw on, there is no agreed-on paradigm for the library of the future. Getting to this paradigm is the task before us (Hartman 2000, 112).

Two factors in particular drive the need for a new paradigm. The more obvious of the two is the revolution in information technology that has been gathering speed since the 1960s and that took off in 1993 with the debut of the World Wide Web. The second factor, somewhat quieter but no less profound, is the move in higher education away from a teaching culture and toward a culture of learning.

> In its briefest form, the paradigm that has [traditionally] governed our colleges is this: A college is an institution that exists

to provide instruction. Subtly but profoundly we are shifting to a new paradigm: A college is an institution that exists to produce learning. This shift changes everything. . . . We are beginning to recognize that our dominant paradigm mistakes a means for an end. It takes the means or method—called "instruction" or "teaching"—and makes it the college's end or purpose. To say that the purpose of colleges is to provide instruction is like saying that General Motors' business is to operate assembly lines or that the purpose of medical care is to fill hospital beds. We now see that our mission is not instruction but rather that of producing learning with every student by whatever means work best (Barr and Tagg 1995).

Librarians and library designers need to join faculty in this paradigm shift. We need to understand that the success of the academic library is best measured not by the frequency and ease of library use but by the learning that results from that use. Our purpose is not to circulate books, but to ensure that the circulation of knowledge produces learning. Reconceiving our purposes involves a fundamental shift for librarians trained in a service culture—one that is comparable to the shift that faculty are making as they move from a teaching to a learning culture. Academic librarians need to make a paradigm shift from a service to a learning culture.

The dominance of the service culture in current library space planning is strikingly evident in how academic library directors characterize their planning methods. Describing 240 construction and renovation projects completed between 1992 and 2001, these directors reported conducting systematic evaluations of library operations 85 percent of the time, while doing systematic assessments of student learning and faculty teaching behaviors only 41 percent and 31 percent of the time, respectively. The latter two figures are probably overstated. Follow-up interviews with a number of library directors revealed that even when they had reported doing a systematic assessment of modes of student learning, they had in most cases simply surveyed student preferences regarding group study space and types of seating (Bennett 2003, 20–22, 33–36).

The knowledge base that guides library space planning is thus poorly balanced, tilted heavily toward library operations and away from systematic knowledge of how students learn. A case in point is the redesign of the learning commons at one large North American research library. While the library's planning principles invoke the social dimension of learning, the diversity of learner needs, and the wish to foster self-sufficiency and lifelong learning, the information on which planning actually drew was operational: library program and service descriptions and statistics, inventories of public computing facilities in the library and of current staff spaces, and the results from a user survey.[1]

One could provide more stories illustrating the mismatch be-

To say that the purpose of colleges is to provide instruction is like saying that General Motors' business is to operate assembly lines or that the purpose of medical care is to fill hospital beds.

---

[1] Planners looked as well at the published literature on information commons and visited a number of such installations. Project summary privately communicated to the author, 2004.

tween what we wish to achieve in libraries and the knowledge we bring to bear on library space planning. However, it is important to balance such reports with stories about the considerable success of libraries built or renovated between 1992 and 2001. In interview after interview done as part of a national survey, library directors and chief academic officers pointed to significantly increased student use of their libraries as one of the clearest and most gratifying marks of the success of their projects. Responding to changing patterns of student learning was in fact one of the most powerful motivators for library construction and renovation in the 1990s (Bennett 2003, 7–8 and Table 3a). Accommodating student learning was sometimes an explicit goal of a project, as happened at one liberal arts college where the dean believes the library is "probably the most important place for learning on campus." At other times, the result was achieved without conscious design, as for instance at a doctoral university where the library director reported significant growth in group study:

> We're seeing that virtually all of [some 250 tables seating four to
> six students] are filled with students working together, and . . .
> the thing that makes us happiest is that we somehow stumbled
> into a really high-use kind of thing here that reflects how people
> function within their classes and work with their fellow students.
> . . . [This space] will be filled, literally every chair, . . . and they're
> all talking at the same time. And the hum that rises above this
> is just amazing. And they don't care. . . . There's all this din
> that occurs [from] hundreds of students in the same space, all
> working together and all talking at the same time. . . . Somehow
> it just all came together as a very useful space for students. . . .
> We just beam with pride (Bennett 2003, 16–18).

So while we face some sobering facts about the heavily skewed knowledge base that often guides library space design, we can also point to some notable accomplishments in building libraries as learning spaces. The question is, Can we do better? Given the immense sums spent every year on library construction and renovation, we surely cannot afford to "somehow stumble" into our successes.

Asking the Right Questions

How can we get better value for our investment in library construction and renovation? As librarians, we must start by asking the right questions. This will be challenging, because those questions require a basic and deeply unsettling shift in professional outlook. We are unlikely to make this shift so long as space design is guided primarily by knowledge about library operations and only infrequently, if at all, by knowledge about learning. We need to focus on learning issues with at least the same intensity and sophistication that we bring to the analysis of operational issues. We need to ensure that choices about operational issues—the design of reference areas, for instance—are strongly guided by what we know of student learning. When a choice must be made, we may well need to give preference—dare one say it?—to learning needs over operational needs. What would happen, for instance, if the delivery of reference services were designed not around a service desk but around lounge seating? What would be the consequences for learning if the design elements asserting the librarians' authority (e.g., the queue, the desk, the shelves of reference books) were abandoned in favor of design elements (e.g., lounge chairs, computers designed for collaborative use) that suggest the reference librarian is the student's partner in the learning enterprise?

Jeanne Narum reinforces the importance of asking the right questions by pointing to the wrong questions that prompt many construction and renovation projects. To ask first about the amount or size of the space that is needed is to start wrong, Narum suggests. Instead, "questions about the nature of the educational experience [that is desired]—about quality and the nature of the learning community—are questions that must be asked first and asked persistently throughout the [planning] process" (Narum nd).[2] How many librarians can say they started space planning in this way and, equally important, kept educational issues at the center of their planning activities as they progressed?

In truth, we have little experience in asking the right questions in a focused, thoughtful, and purposeful way.[3] Happily, I am able to report on a notable example of library planning that has begun by asking questions about how students learn. An opportunity to renovate the heating, ventilating, and air conditioning systems at the Jessie Ball duPont Library at Sewanee: The University of the South has prompted a large-scale inquiry, led by Daniel S. Backlund, chair of the Theatre Arts Department. This inquiry pursues several vital questions about the library using a set of subcommittees, one of which is concerned with information literacy and is chaired by Richard A. O'Connor, who codirects the Center for Teaching at Sewanee.[4] O'Connor is systematically studying student learning be-

While we face some sobering facts about the heavily skewed knowledge base that often guides library space design, we can also point to some notable accomplishments in building libraries as learning spaces. The question is, Can we do better?

[2] Narum is the director of Project Kaleidoscope (PKAL), which champions strong learning environments, including classroom and laboratory facilities, for undergraduate programs in science, technology, engineering, and mathematics. For PKAL's programmatic activities relating to facilities, see the PKAL Web page (http://www.pkal.org/template0.cfm?c_id=3).

[3] See Banning and Canard 1986, who argue that "among the many methods employed to foster student development, the use of the physical environment is perhaps the least understood and the most neglected." The landmark report *How People Learn: Brain, Mind, Experience, and School* (Bransford et al., eds. 1999), is silent on space design and exemplifies the neglect of the physical environment in understanding learning behaviors. See also Chism 2002, 8, where it is observed that very little has been written that applies learning theory to the design of learning spaces. An important exception, Chism notes, is the chapter entitled "Physical Environments: The Role of Design and Space," in Strange and Banning 2001.

[4] Richard A. O'Connor, Biehl Professor of International Studies in the Department of Anthropology at Sewanee, has been a generous and thoughtful interlocutor in the writing of this essay. He observes that, "the service paradigm can be corrosive" for librarians, just as the teaching paradigm is for faculty. Librarians "do not want to be clerks at Wal-Mart serving customers. Like faculty, [librarians] are people who fell in love with books, learning, and libraries long ago. They want to invite others to share their passion. If we understand learning as not 'what's on the test,' but [as a measure of] how well we draw newcomers

haviors at Sewanee intending that this knowledge will inform planning for library space and services.[5]

The right initial questions for library design should include two factors known to be critically important to successful learning: time on task and educationally purposeful activities, such as discussing ideas from classes or readings outside of class.[6]

Increasing Time on Task

The more time that students spend on learning tasks, the more likely they are to learn effectively (National Survey of Student Engagement 2002, 2003). One probable implication of this for library design is that inviting spaces that honor study are likely to encourage students to study longer. This conviction surely underlies the view, so often expressed by those interviewed for the national survey, that the success of library construction and renovation is best measured by a project's ability to draw students to the library.[7] Libraries are not just study halls; they should be purposefully designed to promote study and learning.

In an independent-study course in anthropology, Richard O'Connor collaborated with five students to learn about the campus culture for study by interviewing students individually and in small groups.[8] The interviews were just one part of their collaborative work, which also included observations and class discussions that shaped an evolving understanding of what the investigators were

into communities of knowledge, then promoting student learning means understanding what makes these communities 'joinable.'" Righting the balance in library space design between service and learning issues requires, as O'Connor observes, that "we conceptualize learning correctly. It is not about providing materials (books, databases—at your service!) but about structuring motive and meaning to nurture the young" (private communication, 2004).

[5] I am grateful to Richard O'Connor for permission to use parts of his and his students' research data. Because he so generously shared with me the field data that he and his students had collected (something not commonly done among social scientists), I became a virtual, asynchronous participant in their independent study. I am, however, solely responsible for the interpretation of the data reported here, an interpretation that does not necessary reflect the views of Professor O'Connor or his students.

[6] These questions resonate closely with those posed in Kuh and Gonyea 2003, an important article on the role of the academic library in promoting student engagement in learning.

[7] This view was notably expressed by the president of a doctoral university, who emphasized that the formal goals of the library project, which he had made his signature project for the campus, were to provide shelving for the collections and to enhance the library's electronic capabilities. When asked about reader accommodations, the president said the library had formerly been little used by students, much to the detriment of "the academic tenor of the institution." But two advisory committee members made it their business to build excellent reader accommodations into the project. The president said that this "has worked out brilliantly. You go to the library now, and it is a very active and alive place, and I think that may be the singularly most important outcome of our project." He described this success, not formally a goal of the project, as "some form of serendipity, I guess" (Bennett 2003, 36–37).

[8] The student researchers were Beth Christian, Chris Honeycutt, Shawn Means, Aimee Rogers, and David Zeman. They interviewed 22 students in 13 interview sessions.

looking for and what was implicit in the questions they were asking. The subject of inquiry was the connection students make, or do not make, between their academic and social lives. Responses to this question revealed a great deal about the social dimension of study and how students managed their study time and their study environments.

In these interviews, Sewanee students distinguished sharply between their academic and social lives, saying little that indicated a deep mingling of the two. These students were proud of Sewanee's strong academic reputation and the way the life of the mind often colors campus social life. But the distinction nonetheless remained powerful, as evident in one student comment:

> I've definitely had intellectual sorts of conversations outside of class, but I don't necessarily characterize them as academic. They're learning, but I don't really think of them as academic pursuits. Academic pursuit should require effort, dedication, and energy. With those [intellectual] kinds of conversations you talk about [a subject] for 30 minutes and you learn something. It's probably important and matters to your life, but you're not going to follow through. And, there's not really anything riding on that conversation. I'm not getting tested later, so I don't think of it in the same way.

This student characterized study as involving focused, disciplined, consequential effort. Other students frequently commented that they chose to go to the library for particularly serious, sustained study. At the same time, Sewanee students clearly regarded study as having a strong social context. As one student put it:

> I think the library is conducive to studying and to socializing; it depends what you're looking for. The good thing about it is I can take a study break while walking around and finding some of my friends who are in the front and obviously not working that hard. But you can find little holes in there where you're not going to get found very often if you don't want to be.

This comment indicated a need to manage the social aspects of study. Other students expressed this need in terms of a need to take frequent breaks and a need for the right amount of personal seclusion, which varied significantly from student to student and from time to time for a given student. One student's observation made plain just how changeable the definition of a distraction is:

> If I've been sitting down there [in the library basement] for hours, the littlest things can distract me. Like somebody talking or the doors. . . . And a lot of times, somebody'll walk by that you know, so you stop and have a conversation. When other people do it, it gets on my nerves . . . especially when I can't join in on the conversation! But if I'm doing it, then I'm constantly thinking we're getting on somebody's nerves. But you're not gonna *not talk* to somebody.

Another student described the study options provided by the library explicitly in social terms, casting them as largely negative options he rarely chose for himself:

> And especially you cannot study on the second floor in those carrels or on the main floor unless you WANT to be distracted. And I think . . . the people who have open carrels are the ones that realize they're gonna be talking a lot, and they're not always in the library. And it's more of a social thing. Especially the main floor. It's more of a social gathering than it is a study area. I'm not gonna do that.

As O'Connor observed in private communication with the author, "we found [in both the interviews and the class discussion of them] that students adjusted the level of distraction to fit the task and its importance. . . . [M]any students have learned to vary where they are in the library to control their level of distraction."

This active management of the study environment by controlling social distractions was also evident in the comments of several students on a small study space in Snowden Forestry Building, home of the geology and environmental studies departments at Sewanee. Snowden and the duPont Library present many of the same issues for students wanting to control their study environment. The difference is that student comments on Snowden are untouched by the faint praise that so often damns the library. For instance, one student said, "I really like the library. The boring environment forces me to pay attention to my work, since there is nothing else to do." By contrast, another student described the mix of academic and social activities at Snowden as follows:

> I spend a lot of time hanging out in the reading room in Snowden, so academic and social come together there. [Interviewer: When you say "hanging out" in Snowden, do you mean hanging out in the same sense that you would hang out in someone's dorm or at a fraternity house, or something else?] Well, we're definitely there to do our work, so it's not the same hanging out as getting together to play video games or something. But we all talk about our work and sometimes the conversation will shift to social stuff, like what everyone's doing this weekend.

Another student described the study environment at Snowden at length:

> The reading room in Snowden is the best place to study around here, in my opinion. For one, the light is good. Also, there are comfortable chairs if you're just reading and don't need to be sitting up straight. Plus, it helps that there are always other people from the department wandering through, so if you need help or don't understand something, there's usually someone around to help you. And I really like the table in there. I like to be able to spread out all of my books and notes at once in front of

me. I can't use the tables in the library because they're all pretty much on the ground floor and there's too much distraction, people moving around and talking and stuff. And I hate carrels: They box you in, the lighting is bad, they're really metallic, and they don't actually prevent you from distraction, because they're all in rows and you can tell that there's someone in front of you or next to you. It's just too distracting. I like Snowden because there's room to spread out without being distracted and if someone's talking, they're talking about a related subject.

One of the group interviews touched on the powerful learning environment achieved at Snowden as a function of the building itself creating a community for learning:

> M: I feel like it's because they have buildings to go to. The natural-resources kids have Snowden, the other sciences have Woods [laboratories]. All the classes and the professors are in the same building, and so you see people in the halls and stuff. The other departments, like English and languages and history, etc., . . . are more spread out in different buildings, so it's harder to just see people around.
>
> B: Space for each department is definitely important. If you don't have classes together with the people in your major, you're not even going to figure out who they are. I think the Snowden people get to know each other so well because even when they don't have classes together, they have that great building to study in.

These student comments suggest that good study space is responsive to the academic and social dimensions of study in ways that allow students to control them both. Such space encourages study and fosters learning by

- supporting a distinction between studying and socializing that does not deny the social dimension of study
- favoring learning functions in the space's mix of academic and social functions
- providing choices of place, ranging from personal seclusion to group study, that variously reinforce the discipline needed for study
- permitting territorial claims for study that enable students to govern the social dimension of their study space
- fostering a sense of community among students, allowing them to be seen as members of that community while they take strength from seeing other community members.[9]

None of the interviewees described study space in the duPont Library nearly as enthusiastically they described Snowden. This

---

[9] Some of these characteristics of the Snowden study space resonate with a PKAL document, Characteristics of the Ideal Spaces for Sciences. nd.

contrast draws attention to the general challenge for library space design: Is it possible to design a library so that it functions as a powerful learning space—one that encourages students to devote more time to study—as well as an effective service space?

Fostering Active Learning

One of the markers of active learning is the discussion of class content outside of the class (National Survey of Student Engagement 2003). To get some measure of this activity at Sewanee, O'Connor formally polled students, asking a series of written questions, including "Has what you were studying in a class this semester led to a lengthy conversation with others not taking that class? If 'yes,' please choose a memorable example and describe where it happened and how it happened." The surveys were conducted at the end of class sessions by cooperating faculty; the surveys reached 19 percent of the Sewanee student body and yielded nearly 100 percent return rates.

There were 169 affirmative responses to this question, or 65 percent of the 260 responses to the survey. Students identified 200 locations for their discussions:

- 86 locations (43 percent) involved domestic spaces (i.e., dormitory or fraternity/sorority space, the student's familial home)
- 42 locations (21 percent) involved the central dining facility for the Sewanee campus, McClurg Hall
- 23 locations (12 percent) involved campus spaces other than the dinning hall (e.g., classrooms, faculty offices, campus walks, a campus coffee shop, the gym)
- 23 locations (12 percent) involved a variety of "other" spaces (e.g., cars, phone conversations, electronic messages, bars, and coffee houses)
- 2 locations (1 percent) involved the library
- 24 locations (12 percent) were unspecified

Domestic space was by far the most frequent venue for conversations about class content with others not taking that class. Food and beverages were clearly a part of many of these conversations. A number of respondents located the conversations at family meals, and the campus dining hall (and coffee houses and local bars) were mentioned frequently.[10]

---

[10] Respondents frequently mentioned exchanges about religion, current affairs, historical events, and politics as prompting discussions of class material with others not taking the class. Students also frequently evaluated classes and instructors for their peers. Sometimes, conversations begun in class continued afterwards and involved students not taking the class. On occasion, a respondent reported being so excited about a class meeting, a reading, an assignment, or a course that he or she would instigate a conversation about class content. O'Connor observes implications for space design in these responses, in that some locales invite inquiry and interruption. For instance, one student said he had conversations sitting on his dormitory porch when people noticed what he was reading. Commenting on this situation, other students reported that certain locations and behaviors combine to invite people to stop and ask about what one is doing. The first floor of the duPont Library was often described as such a space, at least for brief conversations.

The library should also be congenial to conversations that share knowledge gained in class. It is the one place where all the academic practices of the campus are brought together, making it one of the best places for students to grasp both the integrity of knowledge and the idea of knowing as a collective ongoing practice. But conversations that share knowledge gained in class almost never happen in the library. To change this, one might ask how library space might be domesticated. The objective, of course, is not to turn libraries into residence halls. We should instead try to understand what characteristics make domestic space so congenial to the desired academic behavior and discover how those characteristics might become part of the library ethos.

One might hypothesize that the library, like faculty offices (which are also rarely the locale of the desired conversations), are "work spaces" where one subordinates, rather than expresses, self. Restating this point in terms suggested by Kenneth Bruffee, these are spaces that affirm the foundational or cognitive view of knowledge, where "knowledge is an entity formalized by the individual mind and verified against reality," often by a person with expert knowledge of the topic. Classroom and office space design typically underscores the authority of the teacher,[11] just as library space often reinforces the authority of library staff. Domestic spaces, by contrast, affirm a nonfoundational view that holds knowledge to be "a community project. People construct knowledge working together in groups, interdependently. All knowledge is therefore the 'property' not of an individual person but of some community or other, the community that constructed it in the language spoken by members of that community" (Bruffee 1999, 180, 294–295).[12] The argument here is that campus work space, be it faculty offices or the library, usually reinforces inequalities of authority in knowing—inequalities that strongly inform the accepted social norms of academe. By contrast, in domestic space it is possible to manage inequalities of authority (which of course often still exist) in ways that at least partly neutralize them.[13]

Classroom and office space design typically underscores the authority of the teacher, just as library space often reinforces the authority of library staff. Domestic spaces, by contrast, affirm a view that holds knowledge to be "a community project."

---

[11] Faculty figured hardly at all in the interviews conducted by O'Connor's students with their fellow students, except as academic authorities and the source of grades.

[12] Writing specifically of reading and libraries, Bruffee observes that "reading is one way to join new communities, the ones represented by the authors of the texts we read. By reading, we acquire fluency in the language of the text and make it our own. Library stacks, from this perspective, are not a repository; they are a crowd" (Bruffee 1999, 8–9). Libraries should be designed to facilitate "conversations" within this crowd of voices. On this matter, Bruffee cites Bechtel 1986.

[13] O'Connor suggests another set of concepts—"elevation" and "enthusiasm"— to understand the domestication of space. Regarding elevation, "things are right or wrong in foundational space, but 'domestic space' accepts all thoughts as participation." As regards enthusiasm, "being too enthusiastic in foundational space—a place that carries authority—is like asking for extra work at the factory. In community space, [enthusiasm] is welcome. It is a way of sharing, of revealing yourself. I wonder if we should not talk about formal, personal, and in-between or convertible space" (private communication, 2004).

How is this done? How do students come to claim a learning space as their own, as distinguished from, say, the classroom space managed by faculty experts? How is knowledge space domesticated? Surely food plays a significant role in domesticating authority, as it does in so many other realms. It is good that food service of one sort or another has become a standard feature of library design (Bennett 2003, 18–19). However, food service needs to be seen not as an end in itself but as a means for creating community among learners. It is useful to return to the student interview comments (not formally associated with the survey responses being reported here) to see how learning communities are built at Sewanee. The language of domestic space figures prominently, for instance, in the way students see congenial feelings among faculty shaping powerful learning environments. One student made the following observation about the French Department:

> All the teachers get along and if one of them has a question in the middle of class, they can just run into the class next door and ask it. They're all really excited when someone joins the department, even if it's just to take one class. And they get everyone to eat lunch together and have stuff at the French house, and they're always having fun. The French house is sort of a center for the department where everyone can get together.

Sense of community figures importantly in a comment made by another student during the same group interview:

> The [religion] department is smaller [than many other departments], so you get to know everyone. I think that getting to know people happens in most of the majors, but in departments like religion it just happens later than like in natural resources. The religion kids start coming together junior year. Like anthro[pology] kids start coming together after social theory. But the professors in the religion department all get along, and I think that helps to keep things together. That's part of the reason why I want to switch over there [from another major] sometimes. I think the professors are really cool and everything, and I like how everyone knows each other.

Sewanee students are strongly attracted to domesticated public spaces as learning spaces.[14] The domesticating behaviors of those who occupy such space, especially faculty who model these behaviors, account for much of the attraction. Such behaviors are excep-

---

[14] Is it possible for learning space to become too domesticated? This same student suggests so in observing students majoring in geology and natural resources: "I definitely think the Snowden kids are the most connected of the majors. They're together all the time, almost like a little cult. They even sit together at lunch. Today there was a whole table of them, and they were just sitting there talking about rocks like they do all the damn time. Sometimes they make me feel really inadequate because I don't have anything to contribute to the conversation, even though I'm friends with lots of them." O'Connor suggests that what is "wrong" here is that the students are in a public space but are acting too exclusively in domestic ways—just as "the proliferation of cell phone use in public space bothers us" (private communication, 2004).

tionally powerful, as these student comments indicate, in drawing people into a community of knowledge. Thoughtful space design can foster a number of behaviors that help domesticate public space, which may be characterized as space where

- one knows something of the others who use the space
- little is alien to the community that uses it
- there are few threats to one's ability to be oneself, to grow, and to learn
- activities are often spontaneous and responsive to the learning tasks at hand
- the occupants' identities and activities are celebrated.

Libraries are one of the most widely shared public spaces at colleges and universities. Should they be designed as domesticated spaces, in the sense voiced by these Sewanee students? Surely, we must answer this in the affirmative. It makes little sense for higher education to invest millions of dollars every year in library construction and renovation without designing for active learning behaviors, including the kind of conversations asked about in O'Connor's survey. Library designs that fail to do this may achieve little more than making library operations convenient and efficient for readers and staff alike. That is not a bad thing, but it mistakes the library's core responsibilities, which lie not in the efficiency of its operations but rather in the effectiveness with which students learn.

Achieving Design Objectives

This essay argues that in designing library space we attend too exclusively to library operations and pay too little attention to student learning. We know, for instance, that we want to provide seats for readers. To ask students what kind of seating they prefer, or to give them sample chairs to evaluate, while useful, is to remain focused on the operational issue. To ask first how students learn and then to design environments, including seating, to foster that learning is to focus on learning. The latter approach sets right the balance between operations and learning. It gets right the relationship between means and ends.

Studies that attempt to understand the impact of libraries on student learning are often not instructive for space design for reasons well illustrated by George Kuh and Robert Gonyea. Drawing on highly regarded survey data gathered for more than 20 years, they conclude that

> library experiences of undergraduates *positively relate* to select educationally purposeful activities, such as using computing and information technology and interacting with faculty members. Those students who more frequently use the library reflect a studious work ethic and engage in academically challenging tasks that require higher-order thinking. Although certain student background characteristics (race, major, year in school,

transfer status, access to computers) affect the nature and frequency of students' library activities, the library appears to be a positive learning environment for all students, especially members of historically underrepresented groups. At the same time, library use does not appear to *contribute directly* to gains in information literacy and other desirable [educational] outcomes [emphasis added].

The difference here is between correlation and causation. Looking at student behaviors that register in library operations, one discovers a correlation between use of the library and successful learning, but one does not find evidence that engagement with these library operations *causes* desirable educational outcomes. The situation facing librarians and library space designers is the same as that confronting faculty. There surely is a correlation between good lectures and effective learning, but there is little evidence that lectures cause learning. Kuh and Gonyea note that the situation regarding libraries "is not surprising, as rarely does any single experience or set of activities during college affect student learning and personal development one way or the other; rather, what is most important to college impact is the nature and breadth of a student's experiences over an extended period" (Kuh and Gonyea 2003, 269–270).

The character of the study environment matters immensely, and that environment must in direct and tangible ways foster effective learning. This essay argues that space that allows students to manage the social dimensions of learning, that domesticates the foundational character of knowledge (the character that dominates at most colleges and universities), and that celebrates the communal (i.e., the nonfoundational) character of knowledge will indeed foster learning.[15]

Good planning can produce striking results. The most dramatic planning accomplishment of academic libraries over the past decade or so has been the creation of wonderfully rich digital information resources for readers. Information commons are a principal architectural expression of this achievement, and they have even spawned their own professional literature.[16] Academic libraries have no comparable record of creating wonderful learning spaces. Aside from the provision of group study space, libraries have acted as if the challenge of creating excellent learning spaces would be met, if at all, elsewhere on campus. The self-directed student learning discussed in this essay has not inspired library design or propagated a professional literature in the way that digital technology has inspired the information commons.[17] As long as this imbalance persists in our concep-

> *Space that allows students to manage the social dimensions of learning, that domesticates the foundational character of knowledge, and that celebrates the communal character of knowledge will indeed foster learning.*

---

[15] The word *foster*, rather than *cause*, is used to avoid a deterministic view of space design. The view espoused here is architectural or environmental probabilism, where design features make certain behaviors likely (Strange and Banning 2001, 13–15).

[16] See, for instance, Beagle 1999 and Information Commons, a Web site that contains a useful bibliography.

[17] There is, of course, a rich literature on information literacy. Information literacy is often conceived of as a library service, and it has engendered no architectural response except for the provision of electronic classrooms.

tion of libraries and in our ambitions for them, academic libraries will continue to accommodate learning rather haphazardly—sometimes stumbling into success (to use the words of the library director quoted earlier) and sometimes not. We will change our record of lopsided accomplishment only when we begin systematically to build an understanding of how students learn and apply that knowledge with at least as much purpose as we apply our knowledge of library operations. We know how to design library space that is operationally convenient and efficient. There is ultimately nothing but our own inattention that prevents us from designing library space that fosters effective learning.

The argument that we must domesticate the public spaces of libraries and enable students to manage the social dimensions of learning in library space employs some ideas and words not frequently encountered in the literature of library design. These ideas are incomplete, and the words are likely to be inadequate for what we need to do. The chief merit of these ideas and words is that they come from listening to students who were asked not operational questions but questions about how they learn. The listening involved only a handful of students at just one institution; without question, there are other voices to be heard and much else to be learned. One can only hope that any dissatisfaction prompted by the arguments of this essay will engender other, more-instructive inquiries into student learning. We must not just fall back comfortably on what we know of library operations. As Hartman (2000, 112) cautions, "While there is a long tradition to draw on, there is no agreed-on paradigm for the library of the future. Getting to this paradigm is the task before us." The tradition to which Hartman points builds primarily on knowledge about how libraries operate. There is no paradigm for the academic library of the future because we have not yet brought what we know of student learning to bear on library design. When we do so, we will be able to align library operations and library space with the fundamental learning missions of the colleges and universities that sponsor them. It is by realigning libraries with institutional mission that the paradigm for the future will be found.

References

Banning, James H. and M. R. Canard. 1986. The Physical Environment Supports Student Development. *Campus Ecologist* 4: 1–3.

Barr, Robert B., and John Tagg. 1995. From Teaching to Learning—A New Paradigm for Undergraduate Education. *Change* 17 (November/December): 12–25.

Beagle, Donald. 1999. Conceptualizing an Information Commons. *Journal of Academic Librarianship* 25: 82–89.

Bechtel, Joan M. 1986. Conversation: A New Paradigm for Librarianship. *College & Research Libraries* 47(3): 210–224.

Bennett, Scott. 2003. *Libraries Designed for Learning*. Washington, D.C.: Council on Library and Information Resources.

Bransford, John D., Ann L. Brown, and Rodney R. Cocking, eds. 1999. *How People Learn: Brain, Mind, Experience, and School*. Washington, D.C.: National Academy Press.

Bruffee, Kenneth A. 1999. *Collaborative Learning: Higher Education, Interdependence, and the Authority of Knowledge*. 2nd ed. Baltimore, Md.: Johns Hopkins University Press.

Characteristics of the Ideal Spaces for Sciences. nd. A Project Kaleidoscope document available at http://www.pkal.org/template2.cfm?c_id=598.

Chism, Nancy Van Note. 2002. A Tale of Two Classrooms, in *The Importance of Physical Space in Creating Supportive Learning Environments*. Edited by Chism and Deborah J. Bickford, in the series titled New Directions for Teaching and Learning, No. 29. San Francisco: Jossey-Bass.

Hartman, C. W. 2000. Memory Palace, Place of Refuge, Coney Island of the Mind: The Evolving Roles of the Library in the Late 20th Century. *Research Strategies* 17:107–121.

Information Commons: a directory of innovative services and resources in academic libraries. nd. A Web site available at http://www.brookdale.cc.nj.us/library/infocommons/ic_home.html.

Kuh, George D., and Robert M. Gonyea. 2003. The Role of the Academic Library in Promoting Student Engagement in Learning. *College & Research Libraries* 64 (July): 256–282.

Narum, Jeanne. nd. Building Communities: Asking the Right Questions. A PKAL document available at http://www.pkal.org/documents/Building%20Communities%20-%20Asking%20the%20Right%20Questions.pdf.

National Survey of Student Engagement. 2002. 2002 Psychometric Framework. Bloomington, Ind.: National Survey of Student Engagement. Available at http://www.indiana.edu/~nsse/html/psychometric_framework_2002.htm.

National Survey of Student Engagement. 2003. NSSE 2003 Annual Report. Blomington, Ind.: National Survey of Student Engagement. Available at http://www/iub.edu/~nsse/2003_annual_report/pdf/NSSE_2003_Annual_Report.pdf.

Strange, C. Carney, and James H. Banning. 2001. *Educating by Design: Creating Campus Learning Environments that Work*. San Francisco: Jossey-Bass.

From the Ashes of Alexandria:

What's Happening in the College Library?

Sam Demas

Creating the New Alexandrias

For several generations, academic librarians were primarily preoccupied with the role of their library buildings as portals to information, print and later digital.[1] In recent years, we have reawakened to the fact that libraries are fundamentally about people—how they learn, how they use information, and how they participate in the life of a learning community. As a result, we are beginning to design libraries that seek to restore parts of the library's historic role as an institution of learning, culture, and intellectual community.

The design of public and academic libraries is beginning to embody an egalitarian renaissance of the ideal of the *Mouseion* at Alexandria. Generally remembered as the Library of Alexandria, the *Mouseion* was indeed a great synoptic collection. However, its larger purpose is lost from popular memory and is indeed largely missing from our conception of the library in higher education today. The "temple of the muses" was a research center, a museum, and a venue for celebrating the arts, inquiry, and scholarship.[2] Until recently, this ancient ideal of libraries as ecumenical centers of art, culture, research, and learning was preserved primarily in the great, freestanding national libraries and private research libraries of the world. Within the academy, by contrast, libraries became dry, technical, and isolated shadows of their legendary progenitor.

---

1 In his CLIR report *Libraries Designed for Learning* (2003), Scott Bennett found that "most planning was based on assessment of library operations, without any systematic assessment of the modes of student learning and of faculty teaching . . . and that the research process remained primarily extrapolative, responding strongly to traditional needs and ideas of library services."

2 The *Bibliotheca Alexandrina*, opened in 2002 and designed by Snohetta/Hamza Consortium, is an architecturally spectacular resurrection of this concept. Its collections and activities are the nucleus around which operate a theater, three museums, six art galleries, seven research centers, and gardens.

But things have changed. Academic libraries of the twenty-first century—as they reinvent themselves in response to digital libraries and to changes in learning and teaching—are revisiting and updating parts of this historic ideal. This essay is not a reactionary call for a return to Alexandria; it does not reject the incredible advances in information technology and call for a return to simpler times. Rather, it suggests that the college library look to the *Mouseion* as one model for further integrating itself into the community it serves and for providing a unique cultural center that inspires, supports, and contextualizes its users' engagement with scholarship.

The promise of digital libraries speaks to one key part of the Alexandrian ideal: to provide access to a "universal collection." College library collections have experienced dramatic expansion of scope and depth through access to a wealth of databases and e-journals. Another facet of the ideal is the creation of special places in which collaborative learning and research, and creative work generally, take place. The *Mouseion* hosted 30 scholars in residence; provided spaces and services to support research, discussion, performance and artistic expression; and was a magnet for scholars throughout the classical world. Academic libraries are evolving to more actively support the social dimensions of information and learning. They are creating welcoming spaces, explicitly associated with tolerance and culture, for social interaction and intellectual discourse.

As I will illustrate in this very personal and local essay, I believe that college libraries are on their way to becoming the "new Alexandrias" of their campuses. Based in large part on what is happening at Carleton College's Gould Library, the essay summarizes our experimentation in creating a sense of place befitting a highly academic, residential learning community. It is largely anecdotal, based on watching and conversing with library patrons, supplemented with studies of user behavior and perceptions.[3] The essay begins with observations about what people actually do when they visit a college library and about how college libraries are responding to users' activities. It concludes with some thoughts on library and museum collaboration.

There is a growing literature on "library as place" and a lively, nuanced debate within the library profession about library futures.[4] My fellow librarians and most faculty members will therefore find little that is new here. The audience I have in mind is policy makers, administrators, trustees, parents, and others who rarely spend time in college libraries but who have an interest in the future of libraries and in how colleges set priorities and allocate resources.

---

3 Our library has learned a great deal about library use through various assessment activities, including LibQUAL+ and local surveys, interviews with students and faculty, focus groups, and architectural-planning discussions related to a library renovation. In addition, I conducted personal research during my first few years at Carleton, living in an apartment in a campus dormitory to get to know my constituents. I wandered the campus and visited the library at night, chatting with students and trying to understand how, when, and where they studied and what they wanted and needed to work outside the classroom.

4 Some notable treatments of library as place may be found in Shill and Tonner 2003; Shill and Tonner 2004; Bennett 2003; Ransheen 2002; Fister 2004; and Demas and Scherer 2002.

Why Do People Come to Libraries?

Our success in building the virtual library makes it increasingly unnecessary for people to visit the physical library to meet most of their day-to-day information needs. Why, then, are public libraries and well-designed and well-maintained academic libraries as busy as ever, onsite and online?[5] There are still more libraries than McDonald's restaurants in this country, and three times as many people visit libraries as go to the movies in a year (Weigand 2000). Libraries are among the most heavily used buildings on campus at many colleges. If this is so, then why are librarians on the defensive? Why do they sometimes fall into the trap of seeming to do anything they can to get people in the door?

Well into the 1990s, a persistent cluster of popular myths clouded visioning about library futures. These myths centered on the theme that technology is rendering the library obsolete, and that anyone who believed otherwise (e.g., librarians) simply didn't understand the transformative power of the Web. In the euphoric early days of the information revolution, many people believed that we were on the verge of a paperless society,[6] and that the Internet would replace books and result in "deserted libraries."[7] A kind of siege mentality developed in the library profession, reinforcing a narrow view of libraries as being solely about access to information. Some librarians felt threatened by the promise of digital libraries; indeed, some seemed to fear being stereotyped as curators of "mausoleums of the book." Discussion about library as place and about the larger cultural and educational role of academic libraries was marginalized by many librarians' determination to "get with the digital program."

These myths were a function of the hype around truly remarkable emerging information technologies. They reflected an assumption that the inevitable decrease in the dominance of print in library collections would be accompanied by a diminution in the importance of the place and of the profession historically associated with the storage of print. These myths are rapidly giving way to a more nuanced conversation about the future of libraries, and that conversation has begun to shape new approaches to library design.

[5] The important pair of articles by Shill and Tonner (2003, 2004) report the results of empirical research on the impact of building improvements on the use of physical facilities, clearly demonstrating that updating and improving libraries is essential to ensuring that they meet the needs of patrons (and therefore continue to be used and useful) as scholarly communication and pedagogy change. In terms of online use, libraries are finally beginning to measure the use of their virtual services and resources; while the results are partial and largely unreported, it is clear that increases in the use of library e-resources dwarf the reductions in circulation of print materials by orders of magnitude.

[6] F. W. Lancaster, who seems to have coined the term "paperless society," wrote an interesting piece decrying the dehumanizing effect of technology on library services (Lancaster 1999).

[7] Scott Carlson's article "The Deserted Library" (2001) touched off a rich discussion on the role of "library as place" and on how libraries measure use and what factors affect use. This was a great stimulus to efforts to look more closely at what students actually want from their libraries and what they do while there.

Libraries remain valued places of community and of learning and teaching. People continue to come to libraries because they
- offer security, comfort, and quiet;
- are free and commercial-free;
- provide a place to be with other people in a learning/cultural environment;
- offer opportunities to learn, search, inquire, and recreate; and
- afford opportunities for choice and serendipity.

These reasons coexist and overlap. The variety and combination of resources, services, spaces, and activities renders the library a destination of academic adventure and serendipitous discovery. This is evident when one looks closely at what is happening in a college library.

What's Happening in the College Library?

From survey data we know that 36 percent of Carleton students use the Gould Library daily and that an additional 50 percent use it at least once a week. We estimate average student library use at three to four times a week, with an average visit lasting two-and-a-half to three hours. Gate counts show that an average of 1,150 people enter the library daily during the school year in a community of 1,610 students in residence and about 600 faculty and staff.[8] The library is busiest Sunday through Thursday evenings, when competition for the 450 seats[9] can be intense. Reflecting the ethos of the college, Gould is the largest building on campus. Only the student union is more heavily used.

People who rarely visit good college libraries may wonder why students would go to the library when they have so many other choices. Their dorms and classrooms are fully wired or wireless, and classrooms and labs are open for study in the evening, so why go to the library? The fact is that students today are multitaskers, engaging in simultaneous activities and relishing a variety of stimuli. They come to the library to do many different things, all of which support in some way sustained engagement with academic work.

Following are a personal typology and case study of what students actually do in the Carleton library. In addition to outlining major student activities, each section describes how Carleton, and, in some instances, other college libraries, are responding to student needs and behaviors.

Students today are multitaskers, engaging in simultaneous activities and relishing a variety of stimuli. They come to the library to do many different things, all of which support in some way sustained engagement with academic work.

---

[8] Following a typical pattern, gate count at the Carleton library increased significantly in the wake of building improvements, then dipped slightly and is now holding steady at 285,147 per year. Patterns of use are changing. While aggregate circulation of print materials declined by 26 percent over the past decade, interlibrary loan increased by 448 percent. The use of full text e-resources has increased by 1,328 percent in the past four years.

[9] This is the theoretical seating capacity; but realistically it is probably one-third less. While students like social study settings, the need for "personal space" in seating choices dictates that many chairs in a grouping will never be occupied as they are, in effect, part of the personal space of the person sitting next to an empty chair.

Reading and Relaxing in Safety and in Quiet

Daydreaming, contemplation, thinking, reading, and, yes, sleeping are cherished private, even intimate, aspects of the student experience supported by the library. Where does one go for peace and quiet? This is an important question for people who read and think. Some students are beginning to ask for places in the library without the distraction of computer keyboards, printer sounds, and cell phones. Faculty and staff come to the library to browse the new books and journals, and college staff members frequently spend part of their lunch breaks reading in the library. Even people who do not use the library love the idea of a quiet public sanctuary awaiting a time when they can indulge in browsing and reading.

Many students, especially those coming from high schools with stringent security measures, value public spaces in which they can relax and read without worrying for their safety. As libraries lengthen their hours to accommodate student work habits, they are paying more attention to the safety and security of their patrons.

One of the powerful attractions of libraries is the unique pleasure of being alone, in a quiet place, while simultaneously being in a public place associated with scholarship. Students clearly appreciate the fact that it is socially acceptable to be alone in the library. Interacting with others is possible, but optional.

More-comfortable lounge seating, couches, ottomans, and pillows are supplied to accommodate these activities. Disconcertingly, we find ourselves called upon by students to employ the librarian's stereotypical "Shh . . ." to make these quiet activities possible in a community space.

Individual Study

Student focus groups and anecdotal evidence portray individual study as both a private and a communal act. Students associate the library with the privilege of being part of a scholarly community; in this respect, it ranks second only to the classroom. The library is perceived as a comfortable, ecumenical, and welcoming place of serious academic purpose. Everyone is there primarily to do academic work; to enter the library is to be motivated to study. Most students identify a favorite place to study and develop a strong behavioral response of immediately getting to work when they go to that place. Dorms, by contrast, are messy, noisy, and full of distractions.

The preferred configuration for library study seating is shifting from individual study carrels (though these are still popular with some students) to table-and-chair ensembles. Nationally, the traditional library reading room is enjoying a renaissance as a place to study in the presence of others; it is a place to see and be seen while working privately. Assigned study carrels, in which one can leave materials and work intensively over a period of weeks, and lockers continue to be popular ways to support sustained student scholarship. The College of Wooster, with its culture of independent study, makes particularly effective use of the assigned carrel.

Group Study

Group study is popular and increasingly encouraged by faculty through assignments. In response, libraries are providing more group-study rooms. These typically include large worktables with seating for three to six students, white boards, and network connections. Gould has 20 group-study rooms and they are filled most evenings. At the urging of science faculty and students, we are experimenting with moveable partitions and furniture that allow students to create their own study spaces adjacent to stack areas they use and in proximity to network connections and printers.

Checking E-mail and Using the Web

The network is an integral part of student life, and computer labs are widely used for nonacademic as well as academic purposes. Many students visit the library several times a day to do e-mail, copy files, and use the Web for club activities and purely recreational purposes. While in the lab, they also use e-reserves, check on interlibrary loan requests, check out a book, talk with a friend, or read magazines or newspapers. At Carleton, the labs in the library are the second most heavily used labs on campus, in part because the building supports such a wide range of tasks.

Finding Information for Class Assignments and Academic Projects

Nationally, librarians at reference desks are painfully aware that many students wandering around the library in need of help will never approach them. Students often function under the misperception that they are good at locating information, when in fact they are unaware of many basic research resources and techniques. This disconnect is at the heart of the redesigned reference room as "information commons" and motivates the move from a passive to a roving approach to reference and to personalizing the contact with expert information support. Libraries are emphasizing the creation of close liaison relationships between librarians and faculty and students of specific departments. At Carleton, faculty introduce students to their liaison librarians in class sessions, and the students get to know the librarians better through library public relations efforts and informal contacts. These experiences have dramatically increased student use of individual consultation services with reference librarians. Students like these one-on-one meetings in the office of "their" liaison librarian, and they benefit from small-group tutorials associated with specific class assignments. This requires office spaces, labs, and reference areas designed for in-depth consultations rather than quick-answer interactions.

Information Production: Computing, Writing, and Creating Presentations

Students combine information from a wide range of sources and genres when producing papers and presentations. They need computer workstations for comfortable group work and expansive surfaces to spread out their study materials. Increasingly, students

Faculty members like to teach in library classrooms because of the handy access to learning resources and the idea of teaching "among the books."

also require workstations that allow them to scan materials; access and edit music, video, and still images; do color printing; and use software to facilitate analysis and visualization of data. These activities require carefully designed facilities with convenient access to consulting support for finding intellectual content and for using technology to understand and present it. Library planning addresses the convergence of information and technology service programs through the information commons, combining library reference and information technology (IT) help-desk functions. At Carleton, we do not use the term *information commons* but we have adopted the model. Our joint service point, called "research/IT," is proving very popular with students because of the convenience of "one-stop shopping."

As part of this experiment in redesigning the reference room and reconfiguring computer spaces, we are using smart boards (computer-projection equipment that supports browsing and creating and editing a wide range of information formats, including Web pages) to create technology-rich venues that support spontaneous peer-to-peer teaching in the library.

In addition to the centrally located reference room or information commons, there is a need for distributed computing resources throughout the building. The traditional centralized "computer farm," designed to squeeze as many computers as possible into one room, is giving way to smaller clusters of computers. Spread throughout the building and placed on more-flexible and commodious furniture, these minilabs contain a rich suite of productivity processing tools and act as a Kinko's-like service center that enables students to find, manipulate, and create information.

Classroom-Based Teaching and Learning

In addition to serving as a place for informal and individual interactions with librarians, campus libraries have become the sites for scheduled, formal classes. Faculty members like to teach in library classrooms because of the handy access to learning resources and the idea of teaching "among the books"; for example, the seminar room in Gould Library is said to be the most sought-after small classroom on campus. Classes are free to move into the stacks, and faculty can easily bring library materials for teaching purposes. Students like the convenience of staying in the library after class or coming in early to work on assignments. Library classrooms are popular group-study spaces in the evening. E-classrooms, combining flexible, seminar-style seating in the center with computers on the periphery, are proving highly adaptable to the teaching needs of librarians and faculty. E-classrooms double as computer labs and small-group tutorial spaces when not in use for teaching.

Browsing

Serendipitous discovery is one benefit of being in an educational environment. We have no way of knowing how many library users are rewarded each day in their print and electronic browsing by an unexpected encounter that produces a new clue, opens a new train of thought in an intellectual puzzle, or provides the missing link in their argument or understanding. However, anecdotal evidence from students and faculty confirms that serendipitous discovery is a common and treasured experience in libraries. Building expansions and compact shelving allow colleges to keep as much of their collections as possible on campus, preserving the possibilities for serendipity in the stacks.

Nonlibrary Uses

Reading, studying, browsing, doing research, and creating papers and presentations are the sorts of activities with which academic libraries are traditionally associated. What follows in this typology of student behaviors and library functions and roles are activities that have been, until recently, less often discussed. These activities are highly valued by students, but are often viewed as frivolous or "off mission" by those who do not depend on the library as their primary place for doing academic work. These library roles connect the student or scholar with the larger academic community in ways that are often hard for them to articulate but are deeply felt. Collectively, they enhance and embody the larger purpose of a liberal arts education, connecting students who are searching for their muses with a long history of scholarly traditions reaching back to Alexandria.

Shill and Tonner's research (2003, 2004) shows that many functions traditionally considered "nonlibrary" were included in 182 surveyed academic libraries built or renovated between 1995 and 2002. For example, 25 percent of survey respondents included art galleries, 32 percent cafés, 20 percent auditoriums, 53 percent seminar rooms, 83 percent conference rooms, and 17 percent writing labs. It is important to note that the survey authors found no evidence that including these functions increases overall gate counts. This reinforces my conviction that libraries should not diversify their facilities and services simply to bolster use figures. The purpose of offering what are now quaintly termed *nonlibrary* services is to qualitatively enhance the library as a resource and to create an atmosphere conducive to sustained, serious academic work. The following activities are aspects of humanizing and updating the library's program for students who are serious about academics. They are social and cultural dimensions to a program of engaging students in enjoyment of the larger life of the mind that is such an important part of the undergraduate experience.

Using Other Academic Support Services

Colleges and universities have spawned a host of academic-support services such as writing and tutoring centers, teaching and learning centers, international programs, career centers, offices for multicultural affairs, and academic computing support. These grew up incrementally and were initially located wherever space could be found. Campus planning programs have since attempted to plan their locations more strategically, and academic administrators are continually looking for ways to find programmatic synergies among the growing array of support services. At Carleton, we are experimenting with branch locations of the Writing Center and the Career Center in the library.

Meeting and Socializing

Many students spend countless hours in the library and appreciate an environment that places study in a social context. They say that rather than distracting from one's work, opportunities to meet and socialize make the experience of spending long hours in the library more pleasant and rewarding.

Libraries are a "commons,"[10] both intellectual and social. Every community's "real estate" comprises public, commercial, and private spaces. Many public spaces are closely identified with specific functions and subgroups; for example, at a college, academic buildings house a specific set of academic departments. People who do not belong to those subgroups (e.g., students not majoring in the department and its staff and faculty) rarely enter these facilities. Common spaces, by contrast, are designed to welcome everyone in the community. On college campuses, these include chapels; pedestrian quadrangles; pathways; gardens, arboretums, or natural areas; gymnasiums or recreation centers; cafeterias or other eating places; student centers; museums; and libraries. While socializing is not necessarily their primary purpose, these spaces are prized for the opportunities they create for socializing. People who do not travel in the same disciplinary, social, political, or economic circles frequently meet and greet each other in these common spaces, helping build and maintain a larger sense of community. In a college community, most common spaces are primarily social; others, the library and the museum, are directly associated with academic work.

Libraries are among the busiest, most welcoming spaces on a college campus. As egalitarian common spaces associated with learning and culture they hold a strong appeal. Free and open to everyone, they are distinctly noncommercial and operate on a uniquely communitarian character and business model. Well-run and well-designed libraries serve, in effect, as a form of academic community center.

Eating and Drinking

Students require prodigious quantities of coffee, water, and other beverages to sustain them. Libraries have changed their policies to adapt to this reality and initiated public relations campaigns to instill notions of respectful library behavior. Enforcing food and beverage rules is a prime example of the challenge of balancing conflicting uses in a library. Such enforcement requires students to understand and respect place-specific rules of conduct but rewards them with the ability to meet yet another need (thirst/caffeine) in the library.

---

[10] As used here, the commons refers not only to England's communal lands where individually owned livestock grazed, and to an open square, but by extension, a public trust and resource open to and stewarded by all.

A building that clearly bespeaks its mission, in architecture and appointments, makes this respect for the mission and its code of behaviors easier to engender among those who frequent it.

Borrowing from bookstore and café culture, more libraries are including cafés inside of or adjacent to their service areas. When done thoughtfully as part of an overall strategy for library development and stewardship, cafés can be a positive element in creating a sense of place in a library. However, introducing a café in hopes of boosting flagging circulation or gate counts is a sorry substitute for addressing substantive deficiencies in library support and services—deficiencies that would also be much more costly to correct.

Participating in Cultural Events and Civic Discourse

Libraries have historically played active roles in the intellectual and cultural lives of the communities they serve. In our democracy, the right of peaceable public assembly is included in the First Amendment, and libraries actively support civic and intellectual discourse. Today, many academic libraries host community activities, including poetry readings and author events, debates, concerts, discussion forums, and lectures. The Gould Library Athenaeum, an elegant reading room and a cultural venue open to all, joins with academic departments and other campus entities in cosponsoring cultural events during the school year. The library hosts about 65 events, involving about 2,300 participants, each year. Students studying in the library sometimes take a break to attend an event they would have missed if it were held in a classroom building. Faculty members are grateful for the logistical support and elegant space provided in cohosting appearances by visiting scholars and artists. Members of the college and local communities take pleasure in gathering in the scholarly atmosphere of the library for cultural events. When the library acts as a welcoming and lively host, engaging the community in discourse and in enjoyment of the life of the mind, the community perception of the role of the library on campus begins to change. The library becomes a true cultural center and an agent in community building, and library staff and programs become engaged with the community in more and different ways.

Having Fun

Libraries are places of serious purpose, imbued with the palpable, but invisible, patina of generations of faculty and students reading, writing, and thinking. But staff and patrons enjoy occasional bursts of pure fun in their hallowed halls. Liberal arts college libraries in particular have developed a wealth of fun traditions to leaven the intense scholarly atmosphere.

Amherst College throws a dance party in the library for first-year students—a once-in-a-lifetime opportunity to let loose in the library. St. Olaf College hosts an annual benefit miniature-golf game that has patrons putting through the library's far reaches. Agnes Scott's library recently hosted the premiere of a musical theater piece about a mixed-blood slave who worked in the Library at Alexandria

With gifts from travelers we are creating a ludotheque, *or game library, that invites students taking a study break to engage in interesting intellectual puzzles and games from around the world.*

(this piece will go on to be performed in libraries around the world). Mt. Holyoke's library hosts a student theater production in its lobby each year. These are but a few examples of the fun side of library life. Each library finds its own ways of celebrating community and its role in community building.

Carleton sees itself as a serious place that does not take itself too seriously. The library mixes serious work with special events and collections, encouraging fun in many ways. With gifts from travelers we are creating a *ludotheque*, or game library, that invites students taking a study break to engage in interesting intellectual puzzles and games from around the world. Students post a playful "word of the week" in the library and have offered a prize for the best piece of writing using all the words presented in a single term. The library makes the list of the student newspaper's "10 best places to make love on campus." During study week, the student Friends of the Library group hosts a nighttime study break (outside the library) with hot drinks and snacks. A longstanding campus-wide tradition on the night before exams in spring term is "Primal Scream," after which catharsis students gather in the lobby of the library (no one remembers just how or when this started) to enjoy performances by the college a cappella singers and comedy improv groups. Athenaeum events celebrate Burns' Night with a bagpipe processional around campus and around the library; Shakespeare's birthday features readings and enactments (the sword scene in the final act of *Hamlet*, performed by student fencers, was memorable). Finally, receptions to student-curated exhibits or student art exhibitions are always fun.

Visiting/Touring

College campuses are magnets for people passing through town and for friends and families of students and faculty. Because they are open long hours and prominent in location, the college libraries are one of the few truly welcoming, comfortable campus spaces for visitors. The library is seen as a reflection of college values and as a symbol of college pride, and its appearance and atmosphere play a role in shaping the perceptions of visitors. Middlebury College, in its new library, has established the "library concierge" as a central campus information desk to provide visitors and others welcome and information about the college.

Viewing Exhibitions

In the Carleton library, students encounter a variety of exhibits featuring books and artifacts, artwork, and student projects. Curated by a team of students, faculty members, and library staff, and connected to coursework or campus conversations, our exhibits often highlight library and archives collections and other campus resources. About 24 such exhibits are produced annually, under the direction of the curator of Library Art and Exhibitions. Prominently displayed in the library lobby and frequently accompanied by opening events, this student work is read and viewed by the entire community. While labor-intensive, such exhibits support student work and connect them

Revisiting the Mouseion: Opportunities for Library/Museum Collaboration

Libraries and museums, our great civic collections, standing at the nexus of all disciplines, are direct descendants of the Mouseion at Alexandria. Both have evolved into highly specialized institutions but are still dedicated to the premise that vast collections of objects and ideas, appropriately assembled and classified, are essential to the human quest for meaning, understanding, and beauty. Once closely united as parts of the temple of the muses, the musaeum, the studio and studiolo, and the cabinet of wonders (Wunderkammer) (Findlen 1989), they are now distant cousins, barely speaking the same language but politely acknowledging that they "should get together sometime" to discuss their common heritage and what it might mean to them today. The current climate of (once again) reinventing libraries and museums makes this a propitious time for collaboration.

Both museums and libraries are deeply involved with strengthening their educational roles; redefining their relationships with users; rethinking the use of space for people and collections; creating, organizing, and delivering digital content; and engaging in advocacy and outreach for culture and for new forms of literacy. Both types of institutions are concerned about predictions of diminishing audiences and shrinking budgets. These are some of the challenges on which the Institute of Museum and Library Services, for example, is focusing as it funds a range of activities to encourage and support increased collaboration between libraries and museums.

College libraries and art galleries and museums are particularly well positioned to provide leadership in collaborations designed to connect collections with curricula and to cultivate the next generation of supporters of the arts, of libraries, and of museums. Why? Colleges are relatively small and more flexible than their university counterparts. They operate on a more intimate scale and have close connections to the curriculum and to their communities. Their liberal arts graduates go on to pursue lifelong learning and to occupy positions of influence. As larger institutions are, colleges are under pressure from the administration to find ways to contain costs and to optimize the value of existing institutional resources.

We are beginning to see more collaboration between libraries and museums in higher education, particularly in the digital arena. Following are some areas for collaboration that have potential to advance educational goals, develop programmatic and cost efficiencies, and demonstrate how academic support units can cooperate to expand information access. These collaborations will inform how campus learning spaces are designed, equipped, supported, and located.

Development of Visual Literacy Programs

Librarians, curators, and IT personnel are logical cooperators in campuswide initiatives to strengthen visual literacy—i.e., the ability to analyze and critically evaluate messages within a visual format—in the liberal arts curriculum. Working with faculty, they collaborate in supporting teaching, course redesign, and curriculum development focusing on the use and appreciation of campus collections; using image databases and creating and managing personal-image collections; and using tools for the visualization of information, for editing still and moving images, and for the creation of multimedia. As libraries are redesigned and equipped to support a wide range of information retrieval, management, and editing tools, support of the museum education and other visual literacy initiatives should be considered.

Collection Sharing

I am an advocate of thoughtful experimentation with displaying, interpreting, and promoting books outside the library and art outside the museum. Museums display only 1 percent to 9 percent of their collections at any given time; the balance is in long-term storage. A tiny fraction of the art in museums' storage collections (i.e., that part with distinctly lower security and conservation requirements) can be identified for potential display in campus libraries and other spaces frequented by students and specially designed for the purpose. A long-range facilities program to gradually upgrade the

"Observing, Thinking, Breathing: The Nancy Gast Riss '77 Carleton Cabinet of Wonders," by Jody Williams.

Gould Library commissioned artist Jody Williams to create this Wunderkammer, or "cabinet of wonders," for permanent display. Like the ancient Wunderkammer, libraries and museums assemble and classify vast collections of objects and ideas, a role that is essential to the human quest for meaning and understanding.

conditions in selected campus venues is required for a distributed approach to display of artwork.

Cooperative Exhibition and Gift Programs

Libraries can fairly easily cooperate with the campus museum to display works that complement and promote museum exhibitions. Special-collections materials and artists' books can be displayed in the museum and in properly designed departmental exhibit cases. An arrangement for giving the museum first right of refusal for gifts of art to the library should be in place, with workable provisions for coordinating the museum's curation of such gifts with their display in the library. Library/museum cooperation on student-curated, curricular-based exhibitions—employing books, manuscripts, art, and artifacts—provides students with real-life experience in designing and curating exhibits that cross the traditional boundaries between libraries and museums.

Creating, Organizing and Delivering Visual Information

There are obvious benefits to sharing expertise and joint planning in providing network access to visual resources, and this is the area in which libraries and museums are already collaborating to the greatest extent. Librarians, curators, and art or art history faculty cooperate in offering access to resources such as ArtSTOR and coordinate efforts to digitize,

catalog, and provide network access to slide collections and campus art collections. This often leads to wider discussions of management of visual resources, including the implications of making departmental and individual collections accessible to the campus.

Collection Management and Sharing Spaces

Identifying up front any overlap between library and museum holdings and collection- management needs, however large or small, can inform facilities design. There is the potential for sharing at least some facilities and equipment for the use, storage, and conservation of art on paper, archives, and special-collections materials. On many campuses, neither the museum nor the library can independently support a full-fledged print or special-collections study room or conservation lab. Together, they may be able to achieve more than is possible separately.

In the spirit of the creative move toward joint-use facilities,[11] more schools are locating galleries in their libraries, a longstanding tradition in public libraries. Eventually, some college or university will likely take the leap and emulate the contemporary Bibliotheca Alexandrina, designing a twenty-first century Mouseion for a college campus.

---

[11] For an overview of the creative ferment in combining different kinds of libraries, see Miller and Pellen 2002; Kratz 2003; and Crawford 2003.

with the larger community in an intellectually substantive and creative way. As our exhibits model evolves, the ideas for exhibits and the work in mounting them increasingly come from members of the community. People now think of the library as a prime venue for an exhibit highlighting issues they wish to bring to the community for discussion.

Appreciating Art, Design, and Nature

Students respect and respond with appreciation to well-maintained places of beauty on a college campus. While virtually all libraries contain some art, it is rare to find a library with a thoughtfully curated, lively art program. The 1984 library addition at Carleton was designed, in part, with the display of artwork in mind. The purpose was "to educate the eye and aesthetic judgment of students through familiarity with artistic works of high quality in a space they frequent." In cooperation with the College Art Gallery, and with the expertise of a part-time library curator, the library has made a serious effort in recent years to fulfill this vision for the library addition. By tastefully incorporating artwork, elements of natural history, and interesting design features throughout the library, we have dramatically enhanced the power and pleasure of place in the library. With as many students visiting the library in a week as visit the gallery in a year, we are dramatically increasing students' exposure to art. Students enjoy perusing the works on display throughout the building and increasingly use their enjoyment of particular works as one of their criteria for selecting a favorite place to study.

A striking trend in library design today is the inclusion of decorative touches that give spaces a sense of warmth, style, history, and locality. These include fireplaces, the use of local materials for floors and countertops, decorative stairwells, globes, ceiling paintings, busts, quotations, and elegant, but comfortable, reading rooms. The artful use of plants and natural light, care in opening and preserving views to the outside, and display of natural history objects (for example, we have on display a remarkable stuffed emperor penguin with ties to our institutional history as well as a prized topaz owned by the college) give a library a sense of life and of connection to the natural world.

The inclusion of art and artifacts in the library harks back to the *Mouseion* and looks forward to a celebration of the liberal arts in an era of increasing specialization and alienation. We recently commemorated this connection by dedicating a commissioned work by our first artist in residence, Jody Williams, who graduated from Carlton in 1978. Her "Observing, Thinking, Breathing: The Nancy Gast Riss '77 Carleton Cabinet of Wonders," is a book artist's rendition of the *Wunderkammer*. These eclectic ancestors of the museum, like libraries, are catalogs and cabinets of wondrous objects that have been assembled to enliven the imagination, stimulate research, and evoke discourse and discovery. The Carleton Cabinet, containing tiny books and objects, is permanently installed in the heart of the library—the reference room. It is both the artist's personal depiction of her experience at Carleton and an embodiment of something universal about the experience of the liberal arts.

Conclusion

The *Mouseion* at Alexandria created an atmosphere and a set of intellectual resources conducive to teaching, research, discussion, and appreciation of knowledge across the disciplines. This maps closely with collegiate aspirations to nourish intellectual curiosity, support independent learning, and encourage interdisciplinary thinking. The ideal of the *Mouseion* speaks directly to our contemporary interest in combining knowledge across disciplines and in creating a sense of academic community in an increasingly specialized academy.

Higher education supports libraries as essential components of the academic infrastructure, but its view of them is often rather narrow and technocratic. As the landscape of scholarly communication and of learning and teaching changes, it will require imagination and collaboration across the academy to optimize and leverage its enormous investment in libraries. Scott Bennett asserts that a new vision is needed to realize the potential of the physical library building and to create the library of the future. He has appropriately suggested the concept of the learning commons as a model for consideration (Bennett 2003). I propose that the not unrelated, but broader, *Mouseion* also be considered as a model in library planning. Adopting this model in toto is neither possible nor desirable. Nevertheless, the legend of Alexandria provides a useful metaphor for emerging trends in library design, and it can serve as an inspiration for planning the continuing evolution of our cultural institutions.

Successful library planning will involve collaboration among faculty, academic officers, librarians, and architects. It will be rooted in how students learn, how faculty members teach, and how teaching and learning patterns will change over time. Planning will be based on what students are actually doing in the library, on what they really need in a learning environment, and on changes in scholarly communication. Finally, it will engage the community in thinking imaginatively about how the library can best contribute to the cultural life of the campus. If we follow these steps, I think the results are likely to resemble new Alexandrias.

References

Bennett, Scott. 2003. *Libraries Designed for Learning*. Washington, D.C.: Council on Library and Information Resources.

Carlson, Scott. 2001. The Deserted Library. *Chronicle of Higher Education* (Nov. 16): A35–38.

Crawford, Walt. 2003. The Philosophy of Joint Use Libraries. *American Libraries Online* (December).

Successful library planning will involve collaboration among faculty, academic officers, librarians, and architects. It will be rooted in how students learn, how faculty members teach, and how teaching and learning patterns will change over time. Planning will be based on what students are actually doing in the library, on what they really need in a learning environment, and on changes in scholarly communication.

Demas, Sam, and Jeffery A. Scherer. 2002. Esprit de Place: Maintaining and Designing Library Buildings to Provide Transcendent Spaces. *American Libraries* 33(4): 65–68.

Findlen, Paula. 1989. The Museum: Its Classical Etymology and Renaissance Genealogy. *Journal of the History of Collections* 1(1): 59–78.

Fister, Barbara. 2004. Common Ground: Libraries and Learning. *Library Issues* 25(1).

Kratz, Charles. 2003. Transforming the Delivery of Service: The Joint Use Library and Information. *C&RL News* 64(2): 100–01.

Lancaster, F. W. 1999. Second Thoughts on the Paperless Society. *Library Journal* (September 15): 48–50.

Miller, William, and Rita M. Pellen, eds. 2002. *Cooperative Efforts of Libraries*. Binghamton, N.Y.: The Haworth Information Press.

Ransheen, Emily. 2002. The Library as Place: Changing Perspectives. *Library Administration and Management* 16(4): 203–207.

Shill, Harold B., and Shawn Tonner. 2003. Creating a Better Place: Physical Improvements in Academic Libraries 1995–2002. *College and Research Libraries* 64(6): 431–466.

Shill, Harold B., and Shawn Tonner. 2004. Does the Building Still Matter? Usage Patterns in New, Expanded, and Renovated Libraries, 1995–2002. *College and Research Libraries* 65(2): 123–151.

Wiegand, Wayne. Cited in January 28, 2000 e-mail "Call for Papers" for special issue of *American Studies* on "The Library as an Agency of Culture."

The Ultimate Internet Café:

Reflections of a Practicing Digital Humanist about Designing a Future for the Research Library in the Digital Age

Bernard Frischer

Editor's note: This paper was originally presented on April 26, 2002, as the keynote address at CLIR's annual Sponsors' Symposium. It was rewritten in the summer of 2002 for publication and is published here with minor changes.

A Vision of the Year 2012

Let me start this essay with a vision. The year is 2012. Chris Borgman's predictions about the global information infrastructure have been realized, and a vast amount of high-quality information is easily accessible online (Borgman 2000). But our great, historic research libraries, far from disappearing or even shrinking, are as alive and vital as ever. How can this be?

Instead of fighting a hopeless rearguard action against digital technologies in the early years of the twenty-first century, research librarians decided to embrace them. As a result, most research libraries are now outfitted with a real-time, immersive theater seating at least 50 people; some libraries even have several such theaters. Each theater features three highly luminous projectors with edge blending. A powerful supercomputer pumps out 60 frames per second of imagery onto the screen while generating appropriate sounds and even permitting users to move virtual objects around in three-dimensional (3-D) space. Users of the theater feel as if they are right in the middle of the subject of their study—be it ancient Rome, the three stable members of the C_2H_4O group of isomers, the interacting galaxy NGC 4038/9 in Corvus, or the geological stratigraphy of Mars. At will, users can fly over Earth and, moving a time bar, set themselves down at any one of several hundred sites of great importance to humanity's cultural history.

I wish to thank Abby Smith for the invitation to speak and CLIR staff for their help in researching and writing this article. Special thanks to Amy Harbur for gathering statistics about book production in the United States and to Kathlin Smith for invaluable editorial advice. A number of scholars read and commented on earlier drafts of this article. I fear that the traditional disclaimer about how they do not all agree with everything I have written is even more necessary than usual! For taking the time to provide thoughtful comments and to suggest improvements, I wish to thank Jon Bonnett, Andrew Dyck, Tom Martin, Franco Niccolucci, Charles Rhyne, Nick Ryan, and Donald Sanders.

The information contained in the computer models projected in the theater, though in part speculative, is by no means fanciful. Published by university presses, laboratories, and professional organizations, the models are readily available and reasonably priced. They have undergone the same academic peer-review process that has long been applied to print publications. As visualization tools, the models are a powerful resource in instruction, but—since they represent the state of our knowledge and ignorance—they are equally effective as midwives of new ideas and discoveries in pure research. Since the theater is the only place where users can work with this information in groups and in a totally immersive environment, the research library has become, more than ever before, the center of learning and research on campus. The theater is booked all day long by classes, research groups, and individual scholars. In the evening, community groups use it to catch up on the latest medical, astronomical, or archaeological discoveries. The theater is but one of many ways in which the research library has adapted itself to digital technologies, which, far from undercutting its raison d'être, have been greeted as tools that help the library achieve its goal of supporting research and teaching.

Now, let's cut back to 2002. The University of California, Los Angeles (UCLA) is the only American university with such a theater—and it is buried in the bowels of the central computing facility, not prominently displayed in our research library. At UCLA, my little team at the Cultural Virtual Reality Laboratory (CVRLab) has made a handful of models of cultural-heritage sites, and a few hardy souls at other universities have made a couple of models of the other things I mentioned—brains, molecules, planets. But there is no easy way to license a model, or even to find out whether it exists, if you need one. There are no technical standards to ensure that my model of a building in ancient Rome will interoperate with another scholar's model of the neighboring building or with another building on the same site at a different period of time. Nor are there any standards about the documentation, or metadata, that should be published along with the raw model so that users can quickly understand who made the model, on the basis of what hard data, and using what process of reasoning.

How do we get from 2002 to 2012? The central feature of the vision is a new activity—collaborative, interactive demonstrations of virtual reality models in the context of teaching and research— housed in a new space, the immersive theater. In this essay, I argue that putting that activity and space into the research library is both appropriate, in view of the research library's mission, and desirable, if we wish to see the research library flourish well into the new century. I also argue that this is just one way in which the research library might embrace the new opportunities presented by the digital age, which always entail incorporating new user activities and services while developing suitable architectural designs to give them tangible form and support. My message is thus an optimistic one: The research library will survive *because* of the introduction of ever more and newer digital technologies, not in spite of them. If managed well and if understood strategically in terms of the evolution of our educational system and culture, the transformation of the library from the old analog technologies to the new digital technologies can occur with a minimum of pain and a maximum of gain.

The Future of the Book and the Future of the Research Library

The research library will survive because of the introduction of ever more and newer digital technologies, not in spite of them.

Before writing about the future of anything these days, it is well to begin with a caveat: Things are changing so fast that we can at best speak of the short term (the next 5 to 10 years) and the medium term (the next 10 to 20 years). Beyond that, we quickly get into a realm better left to futurologists of the stature of a Ray Kurzweil (1999). So by "the future of the book and of the research library," I mean what I think will happen in the next 5 to 20 years.

When we think of research libraries, we think, first of all, of books—lots of them. The fate of the research library, then, is an epiphenomenon of the fate of the book itself. And the good news is that the traditional printed book is doing better than ever. The same digital technology that might seem to threaten the book's very existence is also giving us "print on demand," making it easier and cheaper to produce books, reissue them, and publish new editions, all in relatively small print runs.[1] The real problem that librarians may soon face is not the death of the printed book but the profusion of new titles, reissues of old titles, and new editions of scholarly books by living authors—all made more economical and practical by print on demand.[2]

Moreover, even power users of devices such as personal digital assistant (PDAs) overwhelmingly say that they prefer printed books to books online.[3] Not surprisingly, a recent survey of professional humanists found much the same result (Brockman et al. 2001, 3–4). This is just as well, since we are unlikely to have digital versions of every last obscure text and document for a long time, if ever. Digital-conversion projects, like their microfilm and microfiche predecessors,

[1] Cesana 2002, 179–189. Cesana mentions the Ingram Book Company, which is collaborating with IBM Printing System Company, which handles printing, and Danka Service International, which manages distribution. The books are printed on IBM's InfoPrint 4000 High-Resolution Printer (which prints up to 666 pages per minute in high resolution—up to 600 dpi). Michael Lovett is quoted (Cesana 2002, 186) as saying, "This is a win-win situation for everyone involved in the book industry. The publishers win insofar as they sell books that otherwise would go out of print; distributors win since they can sell more books to a larger number of customers; consumers win because they have a larger selection of titles; and authors win because they continue to keep the copyright on their work" (my translation). IBM is in a similar partnership in Europe with Chevrillon Philippe Industrie, one of the biggest French publishers, and there is a similar operation in Italy in Trento at the firm Editrice Bibliografica.

[2] For example, the Library & Information Statistics Tables report an increase of 27 percent in the number of books published in the United Kingdom between 1997 (98,477) and 2002 (125,390). Source: http://www.lboro.ac.uk/departments/dils/lisu/list03/pub03.html.

[3] Cesana 2002, 179.

bump up against the realities of economic constraints that force us to set priorities for what is converted (Smith 2001) and to confront the ever-dreaded roadblock of copyright protection.[4] So, the transition from the printed book to the book online is going to occur slowly, if relentlessly. Even the massive digitization project announced in December 2004 by Google will not include books under copyright or the bulk of the world's collections of unpublished manuscripts.

But even if we imagine that, with time, more and more readers will be habituated to the online book—in part because they become accustomed to the technology and in part because the technology platform of the online book is more ergonomically designed—we can still safely predict that research libraries will continue to be needed because they are our repositories of precious documents: manuscripts, rare books, and similar materials. Humanists are known to prefer original documents to facsimiles (Brockman, et al. 2001, 2, 4), and there is no reason to think that this will, or should, change in this century. Even if these materials are put online (a massive task requiring many years), scholars will still find that nothing can replace autopsy of the original document. As a practitioner of statistical stylometry for the analysis, attribution, and dating of literary works (Frischer et al. 1996; Frischer et al. 1999), I will gladly stipulate that digital technologies can offer as much new support to the autopsy of texts and manuscripts as they offer, for example, to the medical autopsies of pathologists.

Three Consequences of Digital Technology for the Research Library

If research libraries continue to exist as the repositories of manuscripts, rare books, and printed books not yet available in digital format, then they will also face new opportunities and responsibilities in the digital age. I see three consequences for librarians, creators of digital products, and library designers.

- First, in the digital age, the research library will be special not so much because of the quantity of information it can offer the user but because of the quality of the experience in which that information is presented.
- Second, producers of digital content will need research libraries every bit as much as print authors needed them in the age of Gutenberg.
- Finally, in the age of cyberspace, real space and compelling architecture will matter more than ever.

First Consequence: The Quality of Experience

The research library has always been what could be called the "high-end" place where information has been stored, cataloged, and delivered. Some research libraries have also been places where informa-

---

4 For the state of the battle between publishers and librarians, see Kirkpatrick 2002.

tion was produced; however, production has always been considered a secondary part of the library's mission. For example, the UCLA Young Research Library has generally received a very high ranking from the Association of Research Libraries (ARL); however, because of its lack of reading rooms, carrels, and meeting rooms, it has generally not been the place where UCLA students and scholars actually got their work done.

In the predigital age, "high-end" referred mainly to the quantity of information. We measured the importance of a library primarily by the number of books on its shelves and the quantity of journals to which it subscribed. In the digital age, information online will soon far outweigh information stored on a particular site (if it hasn't already). Hence, it is not surprising to read the ARL report of a drop in total circulation between 1991 and 2003 (Kyrillidou and Young 2004, 10). What is astonishing is that the drop was only 7 percent: This trend will surely pick up strength in the next decade.

This will not necessarily consign the research library to the rubbish heap of history, because the research library can be a place where users find it convenient and even preferable to access a great deal of the online resources that they use. In the digital age, what makes a library high-end will pertain more to the quality of information management and presentation than to the mere quantity of information stored locally.

Users of digital content may not know it, but they need research libraries more than ever. It is true that we can access such content in our offices and homes. But as Friedrich Nietzsche, who started out as a professor of classics, once observed, a good philologist needs to consult 200 books a day. This may be an exaggeration, but humanists do need to read or browse through many books in a day, and often many books are open on their desks at the same time, as they compare one passage to another.

In the age of the digital library, this is still the case. While we can open many windows on one PC, wouldn't it be nice if we could go somewhere on campus where we could find special digital work environments with multiple screens and multiple log-ins so that you could have the equivalent of 10 books open before you at the same time? And shouldn't such a space be designed with printed matter in mind, too? Most of us live in a hybrid world in which the information we need comes both from traditional and from new media. Wouldn't it be appropriate for the research library to be the one place on campus that offered such a workspace? Of course, this will require new space or a reconfiguration of existing space. But the fact that more and more books are being converted to digital format does offer the possibility that librarians can, in good conscience, consign the print versions of those books to long-term storage, thereby freeing library space for other uses. One high-priority use could well be the provision of the new, high-tech workplaces for which I am arguing here.

In the digital age, what makes a library high-end will pertain more to the quality of information management and presentation than to the mere quantity of information stored locally.

If so, the library, not the home, could become the preferred place for scholars to work.[5] This would especially be the case if, as the number of books on the shelves declines in tandem with the rise in the number of online texts, libraries change their status from circulating to noncirculating. This would mean that scholars could count on finding the books they need on the shelves (I don't propose closing library stacks). If books are fitted with inexpensive radio frequency identification devices, scholars could even locate books that are not in the right places because they have been misshelved or are being used by someone else in the building.

And couldn't the Internet itself further serve the research library if, for example, the electronic catalogs of our libraries, which are now increasingly available on the Internet, were broadcast inside the library so that users could use wireless PDAs wherever they were in the building to discover where a book is shelved and whether it has been checked out? If readers were required to swipe each book they took off the shelf for use at their workplaces so that the central catalog could keep track of the position of each item in the collection, then systems of collaborative filtering could be used to convey that information by e-mail to readers with similar interests who are in the building at the same time (Sarwar et al. 2001). If such readers then chose to meet to discuss their work, their scholarship would be enriched and the library would have taken on a new role that is consistent with its original mission to further collaborative research.

Second Consequence: Why Creators of Digital Content Need Research Libraries

Once again, the need for the research library can be justified simply on the basis of its traditional role. Digital products need to be preserved just as much as books do. Digital products, moreover, may be more fragile than printed publications not only because of the vagaries of the storage medium but also because of the ephemeral nature of the hardware and software that supports them. Someone needs to preserve high-quality digital products. Why not the research library? Several forward-thinking librarians and information scientists have already begun to recognize this responsibility.[6]

But once again, there is a new role for the research library to play. If providing state-of-the-art, hybrid workstations will be a boon to a library's users, it will also help digital producers who deliver their content over the Internet, encouraging them to produce versions of their sites that require the highest-possible bandwidth. But not all digital products are best delivered over the Internet; indeed,

---

5 See Brockman et al. 2001, 8, for evidence that most scholars prefer to do their most intensive reading at home; and see the same report, page 31, for a suggestion, complementary to the one I make in the text, namely, that the research library should facilitate scholars' use of computers and online resources.

6 See, for example, Chodorow 2001, 12f.; Waters 2001; Marcum 2001; Task Force on the Artifact in Library Collections 2001, 41–54. See also the DSpace project at the Massachusetts Institute of Technology, funded by The Andrew W. Mellon Foundation, which is creating an archive in the MIT library for digital documents (http://www.infotoday.com/it/nov00/news3.htm).

some were never intended for the Internet in the first place. They are best seen in theater-like spaces and in social settings I described in my vision of the year 2012. In 2002, the only such theater in an American university was the Visualization Portal located in UCLA's Academic Technology Services. Since UCLA's CVRLab is a major content producer for the portal, let me digress a bit to describe its projects and mission.

The Cultural Virtual Reality Laboratory: Producing New Tools for Teaching and Research in the Digital Age

The CVRLab was established at UCLA in 1997 to create scientifically authenticated, 3-D computer models of the world's cultural-heritage sites. The hard part comes in defining and implementing what is meant by "scientific authentication." Of course, in using the computer to re-create a building that was destroyed long ago, it is impossible to know whether you have achieved total accuracy. Our idea is that a computer model is scientific if it is transparent. We must publish not only the 3-D data about an archaeological site but also the footnotes, or metadata, that tell users everything they might like to know about the reconstruction, from who made it to why one kind of marble or plant material was used instead of another. By publishing the metadata along with 3-D data, the CVRLab wants to enable users to distinguish the securely known from the hypothetically reconstructed, to be aware of current scholarly controversies, and even to empower users to tear apart a model and put it back together in a way that seems more cogent. In developing metadata standards, the CVRLab and similar laboratories around the world are taking advantage of groundwork laid by librarians for the Dublin Core Metadata Initiative and the Visual Resources Association. On its own metadata committees, the CVRLab is seeking the active participation of librarians and information scientists.

Equally important for authentication is to use a scientific method for producing a model. This starts with something very simple—but something often missing in a commercial model of a cultural heritage site: A scientific model must have an author. The CVRLab has developed the notion of collaborative authorship involving, ideally, the cultural authority responsible for the site, a scholar who has written a technical monograph about how the building on the site was constructed, and a cultural historian who can put the site into a broader context. We include experts such as these on the team so that we can base the model on large-scale, measured drawings and on high-resolution photographs of the actual surfaces that remain of the monument. We also want our models to reflect up-to-date thinking and theories and to include all necessary permissions and blessings from the cultural authorities in charge of preserving the places that we re-create. As an example of one of our authorship teams, I would cite the group that directed our modeling of the early-Christian Basilica of Santa Maria Maggiore in Rome. The church was built in the first decades of the fifth century A.D. and has undergone many changes and transformations since then. Our goal was to strip away the accretions of later ages and to restore the building to its original

appearance, which was dominated by a fine cycle of polychrome mosaics illustrating the lives of Abraham, Isaac, Moses, and Jesus. The
team of authors consisted of a professor at the Dutch School in Rome
who had recently published a highly regarded monograph recon-
structing the original phase of the building and two curators at the
Vatican museums—one in charge of the excavations underneath the
church revealing the pre-Christian phase, the other responsible for
the maintenance of the present building. It was thanks to our Vatican
scholars that we were able to use the state plans of the basilica for
our model as well as excellent photographs of the mosaics.[7]

The CVRLab is doing similar projects for the Roman Forum, the
House of Augustus, and the Colosseum in Rome; the Villa of the
Mysteries in Pompeii; the cathedral of Santiago de Campostela in
Spain; the Second Temple in Jerusalem; the English colonial town of
Port Royal in Jamaica; and the Inca sanctuaries on the Island of the
Sun on Lake Titicaca. We hope to continue this work indefinitely,
creating models of significant cultural-heritage sites around the
world and showing the main phases in the development of each site
(including, when pertinent, the destruction phase). In other words,
working with colleagues at similar labs around the world, we hope
to create a virtual time machine that will permit students and scholars to visit the very places they are studying.

It is one thing to create a real-time, interactive model and quite
another to deliver it to our users. We do this in a variety of ways, including print, video, and the Internet. The way in which we deliver
a given model is determined by our users' pocketbooks and specific
needs. The computer model is a flexible digital asset that can be
used in a variety of ways. At the low end, in terms of interactivity,
immersivity, and price, is a 2-D image that can be used to illustrate
a publication or a sign in a museum. A bit higher up the scale is the
video documentary. We can output fly-throughs of our models to Di-
giBeta, edit the segments, add music, voice-over, and other visuals.
The result is a documentary presenting an archaeological site to the
public. We have produced such videos for a number of exhibitions,
including the London Science Museum, the Jubilee Year show on
Christian art in Rome, and the new museum of the Basilica of Santa
Maria Maggiore in Rome.

Then there is, of course, the Internet. We can post 2-D pictures on
the Internet, and we can stream our video documentaries. But we can
also put actual interactive models online. These versions do, of course,
have less detail, and Internet users do not experience them with the
degree of immersivity that is possible on other delivery platforms.

At the top end of the scale is the Reality Center or CAVE,[8] two
special kinds of spaces where users can come together in groups of

[7] For more information about the project, see http://www.cvrlab.org/humnet/
index.html.

[8] "CAVE" is both a recursive acronym (Cave Automatic Virtual Environment)
and a reference to "The Simile of the Cave" found in Plato's Republic, in which
the philosopher explores the ideas of perception, reality, and illusion. Plato used
the analogy of a person facing the back of a cave alive with shadows that are his/
her only basis for ideas of what real objects are.

typically 10 to 50 people to enjoy a fully immersive, real-time experience. A Reality Center has one screen that is curved 166° to 180° around the room. In the CAVE, there are screens on at least the three front walls of the space, and, ideally, also on the floor, ceiling, and back wall (Cruz-Neira, et al. 1993; Basu 2001). Since CAVEs and Reality Centers are expensive and available only in a handful of American universities, it is no surprise that the top end of our scale is also the least-frequent way of using our models. This is a shame, and it is where research libraries might be able to help.

Desirability of Displaying 3-D Computer Models in the Research Library

The Reality Center and the CAVE are two examples of spaces suitable for the display of digital products never intended for dissemination on the Internet. Today, they tend to be found not in a university's libraries but in its central computing facility or department of computer science. This is not surprising, because both the technologies and content are still in the research-and-development phase. But this is quickly changing, and some would even argue that viable commercial solutions already exist. Be that as it may, all would agree that we are on the threshold of a period in which the 3-D computer model of a mathematical equation, complex molecule, distant galaxy, or ancient city will be as commonly used in university research and teaching as 2-D slides were throughout the twentieth century.

But before 3-D technology catches on, it must overcome the famous paradox of the chicken and the egg. Until CAVEs and Reality Centers are common on our campuses, no audience for models will exist. If there is no audience, there will be little funding and little incentive to carry forward this kind of work. You don't have to be a constructivist to intuit that, all things being equal, students will learn more about the Roman Forum by visiting it than by reading about it, and that scholars are more likely to have new insights about the data they study if they immerse themselves in detailed, photorealistic representations of it than make doodles of it on their whiteboards. Research libraries could fill the void in our universities, at least in the first stage of the growth of computer modeling. As there are more and more 3-D models and more users, other venues will naturally develop. The price will drop as demand grows. But at first, the research library may be best equipped, in terms of its mission and skills, to host visualization theaters. It could then become the physical equivalent of the virtual communities that have been springing up with increasing frequency since the advent of the Internet and the concomitant growth of collaborative research in the humanities (Brockman et al. 2001, 13). In economic terms, research libraries could do for the digital publication of scientific 3-D models what they have long been doing for the print publication of scholarly books and journals: through standing orders, give publishers the courage and incentive to take the risks inherent in developing and marketing any new product.

In economic terms, research libraries could do for the digital publication of scientific 3-D models what they have long been doing for the print publication of scholarly books and journals.

I like to think that by embracing this particular digital technology, the research library will also, in effect, return to its roots, for the first research library—the great library of Alexandria—not only housed a great collection of books but also had botanical and zoological gardens, an astronomical observatory, and an anatomical theater (Schaer 1996, 12). In the modern period, such features have been spun off the library, which has come to offer the representation of our objects of study, but not the objects themselves. Given the infinite increase in the number of objects tracked by the modern university, it would be unrealistic to attempt to build an updated version of the Alexandrian library. But by admitting the new form of 3-D representation into the sacred precinct of the modern research library, we can eventually re-create something of the richness of the first great museum-library with the help of virtual reality technology.

Third Consequence: The New Importance of Architecture and Design

In attracting people to the new library of the digital age, digital theaters, high-end equipment, and digital services such as the wireless transmission of the catalog throughout the library will be magnets, but let's not forget the important role of architectural design in creating spaces that are functional and, even more important, inspirational. In a sense, this, too, represents a return to (modern) origins: The first treatise on library organization, written in the mid-seventeenth century by Gabriel Naudé, placed great emphasis on the siting, orientation, design, and decoration of the library. Likewise, in the age of cyberspace, real space, made of bricks and mortar, still matters. It matters, I would argue, even more than it did in the last century, when the measurement of a library's excellence was mainly quantitative. Those elaborate work spaces with many screens and multiple log-ins that I hope to find someday soon in my local research library—not to mention the virtual theaters I called for—will all take talented architects to design.

But beyond the needs occasioned by these new features of my ideal library in the year 2012, librarians need to think more about architectural design because in the digital age, users of physical libraries will want to experience something in a library that cannot be had in the office or home, and that something is the drama of community. Library buildings that communicate and foster a sense of that awe will be a centripetal force on our increasingly silo-ridden campuses, drawing people in and facilitating contact between faculty and students and between colleagues in different fields.

Research suggests that if you build it (or, at least remodel it), they will come. Just as power users of PDAs still surprisingly prefer printed to online books, so, too, typical owners of a PC unexpectedly often choose to work not in the splendid isolation of their homes or offices but in a bustling, 24/7 Internet café.[9] Or, perhaps that isn't surprising. After all, in Berlin or Vienna, the fact that you own a coffee-

---

[9] An excellent example is the Easy Everything chain of very large Internet cafés. See http://www.easyeverything.com/.

pot doesn't keep you from becoming an habitué of your local *Konditerei*.

The ARL statistics mentioned earlier offer some support for this in terms of the research library: Whereas total circulation fell between 1991 and 2003, the number of group presentations held in research libraries soared by 61 percent in the same period (Kyrillidou and Young 2004, 10).

Configured in the right way for work in the digital age and offering facilities such as reality theaters that can never exist in the home, the research library can become the ultimate Internet café where we find it convenient and congenial to connect to remote places. With this in mind, I think that the kind of research libraries that will encounter difficulty in making the transition to the digital age are those modernist structures with no inspiring communal working spaces that are more book warehouses than libraries. As a classic example, I must, alas, cite the Young Research Library at UCLA, where I taught for 28 years. For all the excellence of its collections and staff, this library has no grand entrance to lift the user out of the humdrum routine of everyday life, nor even a main reading room. Instead, it isolates readers in individual desks lined up along the perimeter of each floor. This is exactly what will no longer work when people can get from the Internet their fill of disintermediated rationality and Sherry Turkle's pluralistic self, or, as Internet critic Hubert Dreyfus would more pessimistically characterize it, plain old-fashioned alienation (Turkle 1995; Dreyfus 2001).

I like to imagine the ideal new research library as following the lead of Pei Cobb Freed & Partners' San Francisco Main Public Library, whose uplifting foyer was used to represent heaven in the film, "City of Angels." More down to earth is the new Middlebury College library, which was completed in 2004. Architect Bob Siegel describes the project as driven by a concern for making the library a "social gathering center" on campus. It not only has meeting rooms, classrooms, and faculty offices but also provides enough book storage for an anticipated 50 years of service while at the same time accommodating other media, including digital media. It will be interesting to see how well it meets the goal of creating hybrid and high-end digital workspaces.[10]

What will happen to architecturally outdated buildings such as the Young Research Library? Assuming there is no money available to tear them down and start over, there are other, less expensive solutions. Important missing pieces—for example, a suitable entrance and reading rooms with state-of-the-art digital workstations—could be added. If, as I suspect, the aversion to reading books online diminishes as the e-book becomes more familiar, the graph line trajectories of new books printed and old books digitized may cross at some point 10 to 20 years from now. At that point, collections can actually start to shrink each year, as the newly digitized books are transferred to long-term storage facilities. This will free space in existing buildings for retrofitting along the lines suggested here.

---

[10] More information on this library is available at http://www.gwathmey-siegel. com/pdf/middle.pdf.

Conclusion

The UCLA research library was one of the first in the world to complete a retrospective digital catalog of its collection, to make that catalog available online, and to remove the card catalog from the library. The space occupied by the card catalog is now devoted to current periodicals and to computer workstations that give access to the online catalog and other finding aids. The next logical step might seem to be the removal of all journals and books from the library, their replacement by an online digital library, and the closure of the library itself. Some observers have predicted such an evolution (Basili 2001, 35-46).

In this essay, I have argued against this scenario for a variety of reasons—some empirical (e.g., readers' resistance to reading books online, the greater ease of publishing and reprinting physical books in the digital age) and some logical (e.g., the need for a place to store and access important digital and nondigital documents, new digital products that are not intended for delivery over the Internet). The essence of my argument is that, even in the digital age, some activities can take place in the research library more appropriately than anywhere else on campus and that there is a positive interaction between those activities and the design of the spaces provided to house them. As the activities change to take greater advantage of digital technologies and products that help the library realize its basic mission of promoting research and learning, so, too, must the physical design of the library.

The experience with UCLA's retrospective digital-catalog project encapsulates some of the key features of this interaction: As the activity of book finding evolved from shuffling through note cards in hundreds of drawers in scores of cabinets to searching online, the cabinets could be removed and the computers put in their place. But this was not a zero-sum game. First, much more searching activity could take place both inside the library and, via the Internet, outside. Moreover, not all the freed space was devoted to the searching activity; some of it was allocated to the display of current periodicals.

But this example does not capture my entire thesis because it omits three important subsidiary points. First, there should be new space in our libraries for products made possible by digital technologies that are immersive and interactive, and that are not primarily intended for dissemination over the Internet. Second, the library needs to be the place for the production, not simply the distribution and consumption, of knowledge. It can do this by using technology to facilitate information gathering and by creating hybrid workstations where students and scholars can work and interact as individuals and as parts of larger collaborative work groups. Third, the architectural space of the library itself must be reconceptualized to express and leverage its main advantage over the Internet: the centripetal, community-building power of real physical presence over the alienating, community-rending effects of mere virtual presence. And let's not forget the great cappuccino!

Even in the digital age, some activities can take place in the research library more appropriately than anywhere else on campus, and there is a positive interaction between those activities and the design of the spaces provided to house them.

References

Basili, Carla. 2001. *La biblioteca in rete. Strategie e servizi nella Società dell'informazione* second edition. Milan: Editrice Bibliografica.

Basu, Paroma. 2001. The Virtual Voyager. Technology Review.com (Sept. 5). Available at http://www.technologyreview.com/articles/ wo_basu090501.asp).

Borgman, Christine L. 2000. *From Gutenberg to the Global Information Infrastructure: Access to Information in the Networked World.* (Digital Libraries and Electronic Publishing Series). Cambridge, Mass.: MIT Press.

Brockman, William S., Laura Neumann, Carole L. Palmer, Tonyia J. Tidline. 2001. *Scholarly Work in the Humanities and the Evolving Information Environment.* Washington, D.C.: Council on Library and Information Resources. Available at http://www.clir.org/pubs/abstract/ pub104abst.html.

Cesana, Roberto. 2002. *Editori e librai nell'era digitale. Dalla distribuzione tradizionale al commercio elettronico.* Milan: Editore Franco Angeli.

Chodorow, Stanley. 2001. Scholarship, Information, and Libraries in the Electronic Age. In D. Marcum, ed. *Development of Digital Libraries. An American Perspective.* Westport, Conn.: Greenwood Press.

Cruz-Neira, C., D. J. Sandin, and T. A. DeFanti. 1993. Surround-Screen Projection-Based Virtual Reality: The Design and Implementation of the CAVE. *ACM Computer Graphics* 27(2): 135–142.

Dreyfus, Hubert L. 2001. *On the Internet: Thinking in Action.* New York: Routledge.

Frischer, Bernard, Donald Guthrie, Emily Tse, and Fiona Tweedie. 1996. 'Sentence' Length and Word-type at 'Sentence' Beginning and End: Reliable Authorship Discriminators for Latin Prose? New Studies on the Authorship of the *Historia Augusta. Research in Humanities Computing* 5; 110–142. Oxford: Oxford University Press.

Frischer, Bernard, R. Andersen, S. Burnstein, J. Crawford, H. Dik, R. Gallucci, A. Gowing, D. Guthrie, M. Haslam, D. I. Holmes, V. Rudich, R. K. Sherk, A. Taylor, F. J. Tweedie, and B. Vine. 1999. Word-Order Transference between Latin and Greek: The Relative Position of the Accusative Direct Object and the Governing Verb in Cassius Dio and Other Greek and Roman Prose Authors. *Harvard Studies in Classical Philology* 99: 373–406. Cambridge, Mass.: Harvard University Press.

Frischer, Bernard, F. Niccolucci, N. Ryan, J. Barceló. 2002. From CVR to CVRO. The Past, Present, and Future of Cultural Virtual Reality. In F. Niccolucci, ed. *Proceedings of VAST 2000. British Archaeological*

Reports 834: 7–18. Oxford: ArcheoPress. Available at: http://www.cvrlab.org/research/images/CVR%20to%20CVRO.pdf.

Kirkpatrick, David D. 2002. Publishers and Libraries Square Off over Free Online Access to Books. *The New York Times* (June 17): C7.

Kyrillidou, Martha, and Mark Young. 2004. ARL Statistics 2002–03. A Compilation of Statistics from the One Hundred and Twenty-Three Members of the Association of Research Libraries. Washington, D.C.: Association of Research Libraries. Available at http://www.arl.org/stats/pubpdf/arlstat03.pdf.

Kurzweil, Ray. 1999. *The Age of Spiritual Machines: When Computers Exceed Human Intelligence*. New York: Viking.

Marcum, Deanna B. 2001. Digital Preservation: An Update. In D. Marcum, ed. *Development of Digital Libraries. An American Perspective*. Westport, Conn.: Greenwood Press.

Naudé, Gabriel. [1644] 2000. *Advis pour dresser une bibliothèque: présenté à monseigneur le president de Mesme*. Reproduction of 1644 edition. Paris: Klincksieck.

Sarwar, Badrul, George Karypis, Joseph Konstan, and John Riedl. 2001. Item-Based Collaborative Filtering Recommendation Algorithms. In *Proceedings of the 10th International World Wide Web Conference (WWW10)*, Hong Kong, May 1–5, 2001. Available at http://www.www10.org/cdrom/papers/pdf/p519.pdf.

Schaer, Roland. 1996. *Il museo. Tempio della memoria*. Translated by Silvia Marzocchi. Trieste: Electa Gallimard.

Smith, Abby. 2001. *Strategies for Building Digitized Collections*. Washington, D.C.: Council on Library and Information Resources. Available at http://www.clir.org/pubs/abstract/pub101abst.html.

Task Force on the Artifact in Library Collections. 2001. *The Evidence in Hand: Report of the Task Force on the Artifact in Library Collections*. Washington, D.C.: Council on Library and Information Resources. Available at http://www.clir.org/pubs/abstract/pub103abst.html.

Turkle, Sherry. 1995. *Life on the Screen: Identity in the Age of the Internet*. New York: Simon & Schuster.

Waters, Donald J. 2001. The Uses of Digital Libraries: Some Technological, Political, and Economic Considerations. In D. Marcum, ed. *Development of Digital Libraries. An American Perspective*. Westport, Conn.: Greenwood Press.

Web Sites Referenced

Dublin Core Metadata Initiative: http://dublincore.org/.

Reality Center: http://www.sgi.com/products/visualization/realitycenter/.

San Francisco Library: http://www.pcfandp.com/a/p/8908/s.html.
UCLA Academic Technology Services. http://www.ats.ucla.edu/portal/default.htm.

UCLA Cultural VR Lab: http://www.cvrlab.org
Visual Resources Association. http://www.raweb.org/.

Space Designed for Lifelong Learning:

The Dr. Martin Luther King Jr. Joint-Use Library

Christina A. Peterson

Academic and public libraries were once believed to be discrete entities that had separate missions and served significantly different, although somewhat overlapping, user communities. Today, governing bodies of library systems are exploring how joint-use libraries can leverage shared and complementary values, clientele, and space to create synergistic places for lifelong learning and civic engagement. Benefits of these arrangements include efficiencies of scale in providing technology services, collections, staff expertise, and modern library space.

San José State University (SJSU) and the City of San José opened a newly built joint-use library in August 2003. The Dr. Martin Luther King Jr. Library is a merger of two library types: the San José Main Public Library (SJPL) and the SJSU Library. The new library is more than 475,000 square feet, with eight floors plus a mezzanine and lower level. *Library Journal* and the Thompson Gale Company honored King Library as the 2004 Library of the Year for both the physical building and the cooperative planning that have enabled it to offer innovative combined services to the university and the city (Berry 2004). Users include 30,000 students, faculty members, and staff from SJSU and 918,800 residents of San José. The collections comprise 1.3 million volumes. A sense of excitement and anticipation over how this unique project will work has been brewing since 1997 when a twinkle appeared in the eyes of the San José mayor, San José Public Library director, and SJSU president.[1] They knew that several factors predicted success in this project, including

- the shared central downtown location of both libraries
- the need for increased services in a climate of decreasing financial support

---

[1] For more information about the how the merger was accomplished, see Bartindale 1998, *San Jose Mercury News* 1997, and Witt 1997.

- enthusiastic and able institutional leaders
- the ability to choose most advantageous arrangements for the purchase of furniture, fixtures, and equipment
- an opportunity to offer new services, such as laptop connectivity, expanded teaching labs, extended hours, and group study rooms

One major planning issue was the degree to which services, collections, and operations would merge. Which aspects of the library should be joint-use, and which should be separate? The discussion was informed by the distinct operational style of each library and by how each customarily met both the unique and shared needs of its user community.

This essay examines sense of place in King Library and how it matches the concept of library space envisioned by those who planned the building. The questions to be explored include the following: What purposes do public and academic library spaces serve? What are the distinguishing characteristics of each, and how do they give users a sense of shared purpose and meaning? How do we merge public and academic users in one building and retain the best aspects of library space for each while creating new functional areas for joint use? What benefits do the formerly separate user communities gain from mingling in one grand space? During the six-year planning process, SJPL and SJSU articulated unique conceptual frameworks for space use on the basis of user-community needs. This essay draws on lessons learned during that process.

Martin Luther King Jr. Library as a Joint-Use Facility

King Library is a merger of two very traditional libraries, one academic and one public. It retains some time-honored features, such as central public service desks, segregated spaces for some age groups (children, teens), and open stacks of print materials. The new building is situated on one corner of the SJSU campus and has two entrances, one from the city and one from the university. As such, the library is a gateway from the city of San José into SJSU. It invites community users to explore not only the library itself but also the wider university, including events, courses, and degree programs. SJSU Library Dean Patricia Breivik states, "San José State University's commitment to the community, and especially to new generations of students, is reflected in the beautiful, open, and spacious grand promenade connecting the two entrances. People entering from the city side can see the greenery of the campus at the far end of the building, and they walk out of the library onto the most beautiful part of the campus. It is SJSU saying, 'Welcome!'"

An atrium extends eight stories above the grand promenade on the ground floor and floods the library with natural light. The promenade presents an attitude of salutation and activity, with a children's room, a browsing collection for quick pickup of current materials, a café, an information desk, a circulation desk, and check-out stations. This is where users first encounter artwork from a collection designed by internationally recognized artist Mel Chin that is integrated into all floors of the building. These sculptural works include *True and Through*, a column extending throughout the library and clad in redwood veneer from a tree removed to accommodate the building's footprint. Other sculptural works by Chin reflect San José and SJSU culture, as well as academic and public library concerns such as book burning and cultural memory.

Escalators from the ground level to the fourth floor provide access to merged and public library spaces, such as reference resources, adult services, the Teen Center, and current periodicals. These floors include places for information seeking, recreation, and information literacy. To enhance the aura of sociability and comfort, food and covered drinks are allowed on the first four floors. Most of the library's public-access computer workstations are located on these floors. Group study rooms attract users who want to study, learn, and work collaboratively. Instructional labs provide formal information literacy sessions taught by librarians for groups of students and the public. None of these floors is designated as quiet; they constitute the active library space, encouraging interaction among user groups as well as between users and library staff.

SJSU and SJPL special-collections departments occupy one of the library's main research spaces and are clustered on the fifth floor. Floors six through eight are organized around reading and books and house the SJSU Library circulating collection of 900,000 volumes, available in one place for the first time in more than 20 years. The Grand Reading Room on floor eight, designated a quiet area, is a destination for contemplative thought and study. It is outfitted with rich, modern furnishings and offers an unsurpassed view of the campus, San José, and the surrounding hills.

An eight-story atrium provides abundant light and a sense of shared space in the King joint-use library. The information desk, a prominent feature of the the grand promenade, is viewed here from the third floor.

PHOTO BY CHRISTINA PETERSON

Common Uses of Library Space that Create Sense of Place

Patrons use the library in ways that imbue the space with cultural meaning, shared purpose, and pragmatic functionality. Users take the library space created for them and use it to meet their own individual and collective needs, sometimes in unexpected ways. Planners of King Library identified five types of user activity for which space would need to be designed in the new library:

1. information seeking
2. recreation
3. teaching and learning
4. connection
5. contemplation

Patrons of the public library increased their use of the print and media collections by 38 percent during the first year of operation . . . University users increased their borrowing more than 100 percent in the same time period.

Some library patrons make use of all five types of space; others use only one or two. The environmental and social needs of each activity demand the development of separate spaces with specific characteristics—for example, spaces for silence and spaces for reading aloud; spaces for computers and spaces for books; spaces for meeting and for collaboration. How does a large, joint-use library best serve the potentially conflicting needs of user communities? To address this question, it is useful to examine the comparative use of libraries by public and academic communities.

Information seeking is a common pursuit in both public and academic libraries and is a paramount function in King Library. Public library customers look for information important to their work and personal lives—for example, information on sources of small-business grants. Academic users do curricular-based research, such as searching for scholarly articles for coursework. Information seeking requires good print and electronic collections and excellent reference and technical services staffs. In King Library, the merged reference desk, where both academic and public librarians contribute reference help, facilitates information seeking. Here, patrons of all types seek a wide range of scholarly and practical information. Some patrons prefer to search without help; for them, electronic resources must be arranged for easy use and the print collection must be well cataloged, logically located, and open for browsing.

It is obvious that information seekers are finding and using materials in King Library. Circulation statistics show that patrons of the public library increased their use of the print and media collections by 38 percent during the first year of operation when compared with the previous year's use in the former building. University users increased their borrowing more than 100 percent in the same time period. In addition, users are taking full advantage of collections throughout the library; during academic year 2003–2004, students checked out almost 300,000 items—typically current or popular fiction and nonfiction, language materials, and DVDs—from the public collections. Public patrons borrowed more than 222,000 items, including scholarly books, theses, and curriculum materials, from the academic stacks.

Recreation seekers, whether looking for entertainment material to take home or for the opportunity to participate in library activities (e.g., attending story time, using the Internet, and attending author lectures) represent both public and academic library customer groups. To meet their needs, the new library needed space for programming, workstations, and collections of appropriate materials. Some recreation customers are frequent "in-and-out" users; they appreciate the convenient free parking and hours that fit their work lives. For them, the Brandenburg Browsing Collection in the library lobby offers easy access to the newest movies, fiction, and nonfiction, all near the self-check terminals. For others who want to stay a while and chat with librarians about books, public librarians at the non-merged adult services desk offer assistance. This area is in proximity to SJPL's main collections of fiction and nonfiction. All adult users are welcome at this desk, including university students, who use the services and collections of adult services for both recreation and course work.

Teaching and learning spaces are at the heart of many academic libraries. Group study areas are collaborative environments that buzz with students working together; library classrooms afford a place for learning and experiential development of critical thinking; and public-service desks provide the opportunity for one-to-one teaching and learning. Public libraries share this commitment to teaching and learning by offering space for tutoring, literacy activities, training in Internet usage and resources, and homework help. King Library has four computer labs, where librarians offer information-competence education to students, the public, and colleagues.

Providing a neutral place where groups can connect is an important function of the public library, and one that benefits university students as well as members of the public at large. Civic programs, major displays, and public meetings provide forums for the open exchange of ideas students have read about or discussed in class. The library is a place where patrons meet in a highly accessible environment, where information and services are free of charge, and where all feel welcome.[2] In King Library, immigrants congregate in the language collections, reading newspapers and magazines from their countries of birth, checking out entertainment videos in their native tongues, and meeting friends. College students who may have no other space on campus to call their own meet in group study rooms, at library tables, or in the Cultural Heritage Center—which houses the Africana, Asian American, and Chicano collections—to connect with other students for both academic and social pursuits. For these and other user groups, the library serves as a communal gathering space with cultural meaning.

Ah, contemplation, whose loss is a much-mourned feature of place in both public and academic libraries! Sallie Tisdale wrote eloquently in *Harper's Magazine* about the loss of quiet in public librar-

---

[2] The importance of such community places is addressed at length in Oldenburg 1989.

ies (and much the same may be said about a large part of academic library space): "This was a place set outside the ordinary day. Its silence—outrageous, magic, unlike any other sound in my life—was a counterpoint to the interior noise in my crowded mind" (Tisdale 1997). She speaks for many with fond memories of the library as sanctuary and monument to the intellectual life, with designated places to come into contact with the world's knowledge and to absorb, integrate, and create it. This need for silent place is most at odds with other library uses and as such is most in need of protection. Fortunately, big-city public libraries and academic libraries still provide reading rooms and other spaces for reading, research, and study. The Grand Reading Room on King Library's eighth floor is such a place.

What Do San José Users Value in Academic and Public Libraries?

Academic libraries provide learning spaces that range from the elegant to the downright dowdy, depending on many factors. Regardless of size and budget, academic libraries offer places for students to study and work together; to engage quietly with library materials in print, electronic, and other formats; and to interact with library professionals who offer assistance, teaching, and validation of the scholarly research process. SJSU students are frequently first-generation college enrollees and may have few other places to gather for such academic pursuits. What do SJSU students value? A benchmarking study conducted before the merger showed that SJSU students most highly value support for college coursework, support for research, and interaction with library staff for assistance and instruction (Childers 2002). Informal observations of group interaction showed that students also put great value on social environments that support collaborative learning. They seemed to share a sense of purpose enhanced by congregating in the library: to study, to learn, to do well in courses, and to graduate.

Civic programs, major displays, and public meetings provide forums for the open exchange of ideas students have read about or discussed in class.

Public library customers also have collective purposes, but theirs are more diverse than those of university students. Users have in common the desire to obtain purposeful information or pursue useful activity. Children look for homework help, adolescents gather in the Teen Center, parents want picture and parenting books, seniors attend computer workshops, immigrants seek newspapers and other resources from the countries of their birth. The library is a cultural gathering place for groups that can be defined by ethnicity, age, interest, and more. What do SJPL customers value? A benchmarking study done before the merge indicated that meaning and value center around "recreation or hobby" and "general interest," with checking out and returning material from neighborhood branches as important activities (Childers 2002). Because the language, media, and business reference areas were active, the observer for the study concluded that they were of high value and meaning. Quiet reading and group study spaces were also of worth to SJPL customers, as was help at service points such as the reference desk and adult-services desk (Childers 2002). At SJPL Main Library, the sense of meaning, value, and shared purpose was as diverse as are its user groups.

The most obvious differences between the former SJPL and SJSU Libraries were the wider age range of users at SJPL and consequent collections and services for children, young adults, and seniors, as well as the feeling of activity, motion, and interaction that pervaded all floors of SJPL but that was concentrated on only some floors of SJSU. These differences struck space planners as vital elements that had to be accommodated in the new King Library.

Creating an Environment for Lifelong Learning

Students use the library as an education center from earliest childhood and throughout their life, easing the transition to college.

The library's mission to promote lifelong learning from youth to old age empowers citizens and students to achieve a better quality of life, find enjoyment, and bridge the digital divide. The California State University system, of which SJSU is a part, has long emphasized teaching as the primary function on its 23 campuses and has embraced information literacy as a vital student learning outcome. SJSU librarians and library staff share these academic values, which drive campus initiatives, goals, and assessment. In addition, SJPL has a commitment to literacy and learning, offering classes in computer literacy in four languages (English, Spanish, Vietnamese, and Chinese), in genealogy research, and in Web page design and e-mail use. Accordingly, in King Library, learning spaces are emphasized and include four traditional information competence instructional labs as well as the service desks (for instance, reference, adult services, Teen Center, and Cultural Heritage Center). Integration of learning activities in spaces that house collections, workstations, and group assemblage is essential to the libraries' shared mission. In King Library, teaching and learning come to life in collaborative spaces such as group project rooms and study areas; in patron consultations by appointment with academic and public librarians; and in special spaces such as the California Room and the Children's Education Resource Center, where parents, teachers, and education students gather for dialogue, programs, and displays of curricular resources.

The library's mandate to provide a learning environment to all users has led to the creation of a physical space that encourages both quiet reading and collaboration among all users. Students use the library as an education center from earliest childhood and throughout their lives, easing the transition to college. Adults find resources for assistance in job advancement and career change. Adults who are returning to school share the library-learning environment with their children and their parents. This blend of people and purpose creates a substantive milieu of intellectual cross-fertilization, service learning, and cultural enrichment. The availability of space for both individual and group work allows library users to acquire knowledge on their own or in new learning-community combinations. The goal of fostering information competency and lifelong, self-directed learning is enhanced by access to a comprehensive collection of combined city and university resources and by assistance from a staff of knowledgeable information professionals.

Promoting the Library as Civic Space

Nancy Kranich, a former president of the American Library Association, has written compellingly about the important role of the library as an information commons bolstering civic engagement (Kranich 2004). Public libraries have a history of actively developing community partnerships, educating immigrants for citizenship, and providing access to information, most recently, digital information. The purposeful use of public space by people from all walks of life and of all ages, as well as free connectivity with civic thought and action through programs and displays, promotes community identity for all library users. Several community groups with excellent volunteer opportunities for students—in particular, literacy groups—operate in King Library. Such community service reduces the fragmentation of local society and provides students with opportunities for commitment to San José service organizations and civic groups. Service learning is an important way in which the campus engages with the community.

Lessons from Year One

The first year of operation has shown that users like the library. Visits to King Library have increased by almost 70 percent compared with the number of visits to both libraries in the previous year. In addition, the planners, administrators, and staff have learned the following:

- The regular mingling of all library users, from youngest to oldest, works when building design incorporates safe, enclosed spaces for children and teens and when policies require library staff to monitor usage in these spaces. This lesson was especially useful to academic library administrators and staff.
- Users develop their own quiet study areas through a culture of silence, particularly in library space where the building is least noisy.
- On the other hand, study groups spring up in unlikely places; they do not confine their activities to group study rooms.
- Providing separate spaces for different levels of public-workstation capabilities gives students doing research for coursework their own area, away from the family who is sending e-mail messages or the teen who is playing games.
- Students bring in their families, both children and parents, for the variety of library services.
- A roving-security presence throughout the building and an adequate number of cameras are essential.
- Policies and procedures should be planned in advance through staff discussion and consensus; they should be codified and easily accessible at point of need. This process uncovers and helps resolve different cultural values and helps ensure service uniformity

throughout the building.

- Signage, no matter how well done, is not always effective. People need attractive, accessible, well-staffed service points to help them move efficiently through a large building and find what they need.

- Perhaps most important, while academic and public user communities do have distinct needs, many needs overlap in all realms: information seeking, contemplation, connection, recreation, and information literacy.

Some aspects of library services planned before the move and implemented during the first year had to be rethought because of lessons learned and the significant increase in gate count. "Quiet" floors (where users work and study with low-level, minimal conversation) were changed to "silent" floors (where conversation and cell phone use are prohibited), and vice versa, in accordance with user patterns developed during the year. The automated booking system for most public-access computers (not used previously at SJSU) seemed to present a barrier at first, but academic staff and students eventually came to understand the advantages of ensuring a workstation at a specific time. Group study rooms, originally designated to be available on a "first come, first served" basis, are being added to the booking system so users can reserve them. These floor designations and reservation systems have proved to be an easy way to assign priority to certain space uses, such as collaborative learning in group study rooms, information seeking at public terminals, and contemplation on silent floors. The increase in library use, while a clear measure of success, led to unanticipated costs for utilities, security, and janitorial services and supplies.

Conclusion

In the Martin Luther King Jr. Library, two separate libraries have combined their strengths—staff, collections, technological expertise, and understanding of their user communities—to create new places for lifelong learning, public space, and information provision for the citizens of San José and for students and faculty of San José State University. In his book, *Space and Place: The Perspective of Experience,* Yi-Fu Tuan speaks of the freedom of space in contrast with the security of place (Tuan 1997, 52). In King Library, we clearly see this idea in practice: the security of designated places such as group study rooms, silent floors, and the children's room for specific groups and civic collaborations, as well as the freedom of space, such as that provided by the academic book stacks, in which to explore new ideas, knowledge, and learning partnerships.

References

Bartindale, Becky. 1998. Reading up on Proposed Library: Answers to Some Basic Questions on the Joint Venture between San Jose, San Jose State. *San Jose Mercury News* (September 6): 1B.

Berry, John N. 2004. The San Jose Model: Gale/Library Journal Library of the Year 2004. *Library Journal* 129 (June 15): 34–37.

Childers, Thomas A. 2002. San Jose Joint Library Metrics Project: Service Benchmarks, Round 1. Unpublished report.

Kranich, Nancy. 2004. Libraries: The Information Commons of Civil Society. In Douglas Schuler, ed., *Shaping the Network Society: The New Role of Civic Society in Cyberspace.* Boston: MIT Press.

Oldenburg, Ray. 1989. *The Great Good Place: Cafés, Coffee Shops, Community Centers, Beauty Parlors, General Stores, Bars, Hangouts, and How They Get You through the Day.* New York: Paragon House.

San Jose Mercury News. Feb. 4, 1997. This is a New Era for the Bold. Page 6B.

Tisdale, Sallie. 1997. Silence, Please: The Public Library as Entertainment Center. *Harper's Magazine* 294(1762): 65–73.

Tuan, Yi-Fu. 1997. *Space and Place: The Perspective of Experience.* Minneapolis: University of Minnesota Press.

Witt, Barry. 1997. Joint City-SJSU Library Proposed: Mayor Forecasts Era of Stability, Well-being. *San Jose Mercury News* (February 4): 1A.

The Johns Hopkins Welch Medical Library as Base:

Information Professionals Working in Library User Environments

Kathleen Burr Oliver

Nearing her deadline, a scientist in the Broadway Research Building at Hopkins is busy preparing a paper on a particular protein sequence. To ensure her findings are new, she needs advice on the best database to validate her work. Instead of walking two blocks to the Welch Medical Library, she simply crosses the corridor to consult with the Welch's liaison librarian to the basic sciences in the new "touchdown suite."

At the same time, a breast cancer patient arrives in the Hopkins outpatient clinic. While she sees her doctor, a librarian trained in consumer health information services confers with the clinic's nurse practitioner on the details of the patient's diagnosis. Following her appointment, the patient wants to know more about her diagnosis. She steps across the room to meet with the librarian, who is knowledgeable about the specifics of her diagnosis and who guides her to the information she seeks.

These two scenes illustrate an emerging model for information services at The Johns Hopkins medical campus. The idea is to bring the library and librarians to people where they work and when they need the information. The Welch Medical Library is using its resources to meet the changing needs of both researchers and patients. Individuals in the medical disciplines and their patients make extensive use of electronic information and are therefore prime audiences for the delivery of virtual information and services at the place where that information is actually used. But even if these audiences

The author wishes to acknowledge the significant contribution of colleagues who participated in and shaped the projects described here, some of whom also acted as reviewers and editors of this essay. They are Nancy K. Roderer, director of the Welch Library; Harold Lehmann, director of research for the Johns Hopkins Division of Health Sciences Informatics; and Deborah McClellan, G. Stephen Bova, Jayne Campbell, Doug Varner, Willard F. Bryant, Gwen Rosen, Susan Rohner, Claire Twose, Brian Brown, Holly Harden, Robert Swain, Jocelyn Rankin, Tina Stiller, Ashley Varner, Stuart Grossman, Mehmet Acuner, Kenneth Hill, Jeri Mancini, and Antonio Wolff.

make little use of the central library as place, they rely greatly on the library as a resource or base.

Moving aggressively in recent years to meet the demand for electronic resources and the related need for more-specialized library services, the Hopkins library has employed two primary strategies: first, to acquire all the materials it can in electronic form while working to convert older materials into electronic form; and second, to establish a liaison staff that actively seeks out and assists faculty, staff, and students in their work. In 2005, to further improve the application of new and relevant knowledge to our institution's primary functions, Welch will begin to train a new cadre of information professionals known as *informationists*. This new information profession will combine information expertise and subject-domain knowledge. Informationists will participate as members of clinical, research, and teaching teams.

This essay offers examples to illustrate the Welch Library's approach to information services. The approach is based on the belief that, in an evolving information environment, the library's users will be well served by a combination of information-service roles. In this environment, traditional library-based reference services will be supplemented by the proactive services provided by liaison librarians and, in the future, informationists. While the format and nature of the new services described vary, all are shaped by an active dialogue between information professionals and information users.

Liaison Services: The Touchdown as a Venue for Training and Consultation

In 2000, the Welch Library began a liaison program designed to seek out users where they accessed information and to engage them as partners in developing library resources and services. The program was sparked by the fact that with the advent of broad access to electronic information, users no longer needed (and, in many cases, no longer preferred) to come to the library itself. This essay describes two kinds of outreach services that Welch has developed: (1) touchdown suites—small library facilities distributed around the campus, where librarians and library users can interact in the users' own environments; and (2) multidisciplinary teams.

The word *touchdown*, chosen by an architectural team in designing a plan for Welch's future, is meant to convey a sense of mobility. Librarians "touch down" in appointed spaces, called *touchdown suites*, to meet briefly with users; the librarians then continue to circulate through the adjacent halls, laboratories, classrooms, and clinics. The touchdown suite offers a base close to users that encourages encounters, both planned and casual, with librarians.

The first touchdown suites at Hopkins focused on population sciences, basic research, and oncology. They are described in the following sections. At this writing, three more suites are in the exploratory stage of development.

Hopkins Population Center Touchdown

The Population Center Touchdown evolved from a request from the Johns Hopkins Population Center (HPC), one of several federally funded population centers across the United States. HPC supports research conducted at the university in population sciences, including reproductive health and demography. In 2003, the director of the HPC asked the Welch Library to provide information services to its faculty associates. The HPC collection at that time consisted of 106 current journal titles, about 6,300 books, and other materials, including maps, census data, and the working papers of the HPC. One of the center's most popular services was the circulation of monthly printed tables of contents to the faculty associates.

The library proposed to develop a touchdown suite with both virtual and physical components. To achieve this goal, liaison librarians first interviewed the faculty associates to assess their information needs. Any item that the associates identified as important and was available electronically was selected for inclusion in the collection in the Population Digital Library (PDL), a virtual touchdown suite that would be accessible from any location.

Liaison librarians can meet with faculty in the physical touchdown suite, designed to complement the virtual touchdown suite.

Most items in the library's print collection were found to be little used and of little value to the associates. These items were either discarded or distributed to other collections on the basis of criteria that included usage, historical value, or availability elsewhere. Publications in the print collection identified by associates as important were retained and will be considered for future digitization. When digitized, they will be added to the PDL. Current awareness "table of contents" services were converted from print to electronic format, with links to these through PDL.

Meanwhile, the liaison librarians sought out and assisted researchers, other faculty, and students in their work. They also planned the fall 2004 opening of a new, 400-square-foot space near the offices of the associates. The new space is a physical touchdown suite designed to complement the virtual touchdown suite, where liaison librarians can meet with faculty from the HPC and other departments. The PDL suite will also offer computers and space for small-group instruction.

The library will evaluate the results and share its experience with the HPC, the Welch Library advisory committee, other federally funded population centers, and members of the public health and information services professions.

The Basic Research Touchdown

When a new basic science research building was being planned at Hopkins, the library learned that one floor would contain laboratories, meeting rooms, and a number of shared resources and services for the basic science departments. Recognizing this as an opportunity to offer on-site support and resources, the library's leaders contacted the department chair responsible for the shared support space with a proposal to provide information services. The plan was developed by the basic science liaison librarian at Welch, who had experience in serving the information needs of the basic science departments. An agreement was reached, and a touchdown suite opened in spring 2004.

The basic science touchdown suite is a space where the liaison librarian, in collaboration with faculty, students, and staff, is defining and offering information services. Basic science researchers, regardless of specific discipline, need many of the same resources and services. For example, yeast research is being conducted in the departments of molecular biology and genetics, biology, cell biology and anatomy, and physiology. The services plan proposed by Welch is designed to meet those cross-disciplinary information needs. It includes

- a customized basic sciences research toolkit Web site
- customized training courses
- a partnership between the library's advanced technologies and information systems department and the basic science network office for software hosting
- office hours for reference and training of faculty in the sciences, students, and staff
- grant-writing services, including grant application editing, writing skills, and help in identifying funding sources
- physical space for researchers to use computers
- ongoing assessment of users' needs

Oncology Patient Information Touchdown

In 2003, the Welch Library began discussions with the Johns Hopkins Kimmel Comprehensive Cancer Center on the creation of a touchdown suite. The demand for better methods of meeting patient information needs emerged early in these discussions. Patients' level of satisfaction with health care is closely associated with the receipt of information related to their diagnoses and treatment. Oncology health care providers expressed a need for professional help in identifying relevant information and for the structures to provide that information to clinicians and patients.

A multidisciplinary team was formed to discuss the types of information that oncology patients needed. The team includes a senior oncologist, an oncology resident, several oncology nurses whose responsibilities include providing patients with information related to their diagnosis and treatment, and three librarians. The librarians are the associate director for communication and liaison services and two other liaison librarians. One liaison librarian serves as liaison to the oncology department, and the other liaison librarian has extensive experience in working with patients to meet their information needs. Their discussions were characterized by a wide-ranging exploration of current clinical efforts to meet patient information needs and of the topics covered by these efforts.

The group decided to develop two prototypes—for brain tumor and for colon cancer information—to demonstrate the concept of a patient information touchdown. The prototypes are designed to be virtual and adaptable to any physical location where information is needed. The team has identified content areas and types of information for both prototypes. A beta information structure for the brain tumor prototype is available on 2,200 hospital workstations used by Hopkins clinicians and is being populated with content.

Oncology Training Touchdown

The oncology training touchdown suite differs from the other two touchdowns in that it did not evolve from a particular location within a department. During preliminary touchdown discussions with the education committee at the Kimmel Comprehensive Cancer Center, members of the oncology faculty expressed a greater need for training than for a place where they could go to meet with a librarian for assistance. They described a need for training faculty and administrative staff in software use, information resources, and writing skills needed for submitting research papers, preparing poster sessions, and managing reprint files as a high priority.

Because the library had offered such training for many years, preliminary content was readily available for instruction on topics such as the use of reference-management software, resources for funding research, and creation of PowerPoint presentations. The challenge was to ensure that the examples used in the training were relevant to the immediate and longer-term needs of faculty and staff. Examples might include a demonstration of how to incorporate scientific data into a PowerPoint slide or, during a PubMed training session, the demonstration of a search topic relevant to the audience. This goal was accomplished by partnering an education librarian with a faculty liaison from the cancer center's education committee. These two individuals discussed content, prepared relevant examples, and jointly reviewed the materials to be presented at each training session. During the recently completed first year of the training touchdown, attendance reached 350, which compares favorably to that at educational sessions that the library offered previously. The success of the program is attributed to the collaboration between liaison librarians and instructors and oncology faculty and staff.

Liaison Services: New Service and Project Teams

The library as "base" takes on a new dimension when librarians serve as information resources on clinical, research, and teaching teams. At Johns Hopkins, we have sought funding to test new team roles for librarians. These roles aim to make an effective connection between users and the information they need. A few of these roles are described here.

AIDS Information Outreach at Maternity Center East

In 2002, with support from the National Library of Medicine, Welch Library began working with the Maternity Center East to offer librarian-mediated patient information services. The Maternity Center East, located in east Baltimore, is a community-based primary care clinic that provides medical, nursing, nurse-midwifery, social work, and laboratory services to poor, uninsured, marginally literate women of east Baltimore. Clinical sessions incorporate counseling and education tailored to each patient's needs.

The purpose of the patient information service, entitled Maternity Center East AIDS Information Outreach, is to supplement and enhance the center's HIV/AIDS screening and counseling services. The outreach service provides local and relevant national AIDS/HIV resources in a Web-based format enhanced by audio recordings made by the women's health care providers. Librarians guide the patients in the use of the information resources and answer any questions that might arise during the sessions. The goals of the project are to provide information access, and, through audio recordings and librarian assistance, to enhance patients' confidence in the resources and to overcome any barriers to understanding the textual presentation of the information.

The design of the information service was preceded by two years of meetings and discussions about the clinic and the information needs of clinicians and patients. Information resources were designed to address a primary barrier to learning—low literacy—identified in the needs-assessment period. Project librarians selected Web-based information resources and offered them from a specially designed Web site. A nurse-midwife reviewed the selected materials and prepared audio essays on the disorders most frequently seen at the clinic. Patients can listen to these essays while reviewing the resources on the Web site.

To assess the Web site's usefulness, project staff compared feedback from patients who were given Web-based information with that from patients given print-based information. They found that patients responded more favorably to the information offered in Web format. The project team also evaluated the impact of this service on the providers and the clinic. Both nurse-midwives were asked how the service affected them and whether they perceived any effect on their patients' level of satisfaction, the questions patients asked, and the care patients sought. The clinical and support staff reported that the service was very well received. Respondents stated on more than one occasion that it is the "best thing happening at the clinic." They noted that some patients, after reviewing the information, returned for preventive care previously refused.

An Information Prescription Service

In December 2002, Welch Library launched a second project—a pilot—to provide patient information services. The service, called the Information Prescription Service (IRx), drew on the example of Patient Informatics Consult Services, offered by Vanderbilt University's Eskind Biomedical Library (Williams et al. 2001). Welch Library staff worked with the hospital's family resource librarian and nurses, physicians, social workers, and child life specialists in the pediatric units to develop an online form through which patients could request information about their diagnoses. The pilot had three purposes: to develop and test a process for offering information services to patients through their providers, to gain an idea of the benefits of such services to the clinical process, and to informally measure patient and provider satisfaction with the service.

The information selected by the librarian in response to the request, or "prescription," is delivered to the patient or family member as requested by the provider. The patient may keep most of the print materials provided; whole books or audiovisual materials are available from the Family Resource Center for the duration of the patient's hospital stay. A summary of information provided is added to the patient's chart and electronic patient record.

Thirty-five prescriptions were completed during the eight-month pilot project. Patients, providers, and librarians all expressed satisfaction with the service. Librarians valued consulting with the project team to resolve problems. They found that the IRx enabled them to reach and serve more patients and form partnerships with clinical staff to meet patient information needs.

Building on this experience, the Welch Library asked for and received funding from the National Library of Medicine for a randomized controlled trial on information services in the hospital's breast cancer and pediatric leukemia clinics. The information service will not depend on access to an online prescription form or on the clinicians' awareness of the availability of the service. It is being tested as one part of the standard care offered to all patients. Although the Welch Library is not currently funded to provide patient-level services such as the IRx, the proposed project aims to establish the effectiveness of the IRx service as a prelude to enlarging the scope of funded Welch services. As in the pilot, librarians will partner with pediatric and oncology nurse educators in providing information services, referring patients to them when questions extend beyond the identification of relevant information.

Bioscience Information Expert

In addition to exploring new roles for librarians in providing information to patients, the Welch will be exploring new roles for librarians in research laboratories. This role closely aligns itself with that of the informationist described in the next section. The nature of the librarian's role in providing information for the scientific discovery process is being examined in a Johns Hopkins project funded by the National Cancer Institute in 2004. The project is designed to improve clinically oriented basic life science research productivity by completing the development of Labmatrix, a laboratory software-based platform for the collection, manipulation, and interrelation of molecular, genomic, and clinical laboratory data.

It is assumed that the process and outcome of scientific discovery are shaped by the published literature that forms the core of the scientific record. Some posit, however, that data from the scientific record are often not considered for a variety of reasons: lack of time, barriers to access, inadequate retrieval mechanisms, the size of the published literature and data sources, and the lack of expertise required to master search interfaces and a wide array of information tools.

In addition to exploring new roles for librarians in providing information to patients, the Welch will be exploring new roles for librarians in research laboratories.

The librarian's role will evolve during the project. A senior librarian and an operational librarian will work side-by-side with laboratory scientists, software engineers, and other key personnel; their interactions will define the librarian's role. Team members will examine each step in the bioscience research cycle to identify literature-based evidentiary needs and documentation. The team's findings will be used in the development of Labmatrix. After the software is completed, its impact on productivity will be tested in two laboratories. The bioscience information specialist will help in this evaluation by collecting data before, during, and after the software is implemented.

Literature search enhancements for Labmatrix will capture and update the knowledge investment made in identifying relevant studies. System enhancements may include, for example, specific references to the literature or linked search statements constructed as PubMed-search URLs. When searching in PubMed, one can save a search strategy as a Web address or URL, and link to the URL from a database or Web page. When a user clicks on the linked URL, she or he will be taken to PubMed, the search statement will be executed, and an up-to-date list of references will be displayed. In sum, the bioscience information specialist will enhance the scientific discovery process by helping to improve Labmatrix with features that offer access to the literature or to other scientific resources related to the research and by contributing his or her expertise in literature searching.

The Future: Defining and Demonstrating Informationist Roles

In 2000, Davidoff and Florance published an article warning that clinical decision making was not adequately taking into account new knowledge from the literature. They called for the development of a new professional to address this gap and proposed creating a "national program, modeled on the experience of clinical librarianship, to train, credential, and pay for the services of information specialists" (Davidoff and Florance 2000, 997). In 2002, a conference sponsored by the Medical Library Association called for a similar team role for the basic research, public health, and consumer health information domains. These informationists, as described in the literature, would be cross-trained specialists who have specific content knowledge, can provide in-depth information services, and are uniquely qualified to apply their expertise to domain-specific information problem solving.

To test the value of the informationist concept, the National Library of Medicine initiated funding in 2004 for a new fellowship to train information experts to practice in clinical, public health, basic science, and consumer health information settings. The training protocol includes coursework, a practicum, and a project to demonstrate newly acquired skills. The Welch Library will train two fellows in 2005 through 2007, one in clinical practice and the other in public health practice.

Conclusion

Each case study presented in this essay has common elements that are necessary for the development of information services designed to improve the application of scholarly information to scientific research, clinical services, and the public health. The common elements are needs assessment, collaboration between information professionals and information users, and evaluation. We believe that these elements have contributed to the success of our projects by meeting our clients' immediate information needs. Moreover, each case study described here has provided experience and data to inform future initiatives to identify information services, librarian skill sets, and the use of computer and telecommunications technologies.

Our project and service initiatives have persuaded us that the very presence of information expertise in clinical and research settings has contributed to the discussion and testing of new models for information access and delivery. Moreover, the projects and initiatives described here have led to enduring professional relationships between librarians and the clients they serve. These relationships hold the promise of successful future collaborations to advance the research, patient care, and teaching missions of Johns Hopkins University and to contribute to the development of professionals trained to meet health information needs in the present and the future.

References

Davidoff, F., and V. Florance. 2000. The Informationist: A New Health Profession? *Annals of Internal Medicine* 132(12): 996-998.

Williams, M. Dawn, Kimbra Wilder Gish, Nunzia B. Guise, Nila A. Sathe, and Donna L. Carrell. 2001. The Patient Informatics Consult Service (PICS): An Approach for Patient-centered Services. *Bulletin of the Medical Library Association* 89(2): 185-193.

Related Reading

Becker, M. H., D. P. Haefner, and L. A. Maiman. 1977. The Health Belief Model and Prediction of Dietary Compliance: A Field Experiment. *Journal of Health and Social Behavior* 18: 348–66.

Belkin N. J., and S. Robertson. 1978. Information Science and the Phenomenon of Information. *Journal of the American Society for Information Science* 27(4): 197–204.

Belkin N. J. 1978. Information Concepts for Information Science. *Journal of Documentation* 34: 55–85.

Case, D. O. 2002. *Looking for Information: A Survey of Research on Information Seeking, Needs and Behavior.* San Diego Calif.: Academic Press.

Finkelstein, B., J. Singh, J. Silvers, D. Neuhauser, and G. Rosenthal. 1998. Patient and Hospital Characteristics Associated with Patient Assessments of Hospital Obstetrical Care. *Medical Care* 36(8 Suppl): AS68–AS78.

Hays, R., E. Nelson, H. Rubin, J. Ware, and M. Weterko. 1990. Further Evaluations of the PJHQ Scales. *Medical Care* 28(9 Suppl): S29–S39.

Institute of Medicine. 2001. *Crossing the Quality Chasm: A New Health System for the 21st Century.* Washington D.C.: National Academy Press.

Melnick, D., and B. Rouse. 2001. *Portrait of Health in the United States: Major Statistical Trends and Guide to Resource.* Lanham, Md.: Bernan.

Rainie, L., and D. Packel. 2001. Pew Internet Project: Internet Tracking Report. Washington, D.C.: The Pew Internet & American Life Project. Available at http://www.pewinternet.org/pdfs/PIP_Changing_Population.pdf.

Rubin, H. R. 1990. Can Patients Evaluate the Quality of Hospital Care? *Medical Care Review* 47(3): 267–326.

Rubin, H. R., J. E. Ware, Jr., E. C. Nelson, and M. Meterko. 1990. The Patient Judgments of Hospital Quality (PJHQ) Questionnaire. *Medical Care* 28(9 Suppl): S17–8.

Sheeran, P., and C. Abraham. 1996. The Health Belief Model. In M. Conner and P. Norman, eds., *Predicting Health Behaviour: Research and Practice with Social Cognition Models.* Buckingham, U.K.: Open University Press.

Swain, R., K. Oliver, J. A. Rankin, J. Bonander, and J. W. Loonsk. 2004. Bioterrorism Alert: Reference and Literature Support for the CDC Director's Emergency Operations Center (DEOC) and Investigative Field Teams. *Reference Services Review* 32(1): 74–82.

Afterword

The contributors to this volume provide compelling, diverse visions of the library, its services, and its space at the turn of the twenty-first century. The diversity of their views underscores the point that no single paradigm exists for library design. Nonetheless, the essays also suggest some key ingredients in what might be viewed as a recipe for successful design. Good design, these experts write, is driven by an understanding not only of what users do but also of how they work. The design process involves the active participation of many stakeholders—students, faculty, academic officers, information technologists, librarians—as well as an experienced architect. Good design reflects serious consideration of institutional mission and how space can advance that mission—whether it be learning, knowledge production, or civic engagement. The essays in this volume also suggest that good design takes risks: It is often imaginative and entrepreneurial. The intent of good design is realized, and a library's services are enriched, by staff who are prepared to take on new roles and opportunities.

We recognize the result of good design. It is space that inspires. It is space that reflects a community's vision of itself and that reinforces connections within, and among, communities. It may be an intellectual space that brings together disciplines and allows them to build on one another. Or it may be space designed to bridge academic and public communities, bringing civic debate to the academy and contributing scholarship to the public good. Well-designed spaces accommodate the varying needs of users, and can even be molded and managed by them. Equally important, such spaces can be easily retooled to meet future needs. It enables librarians to devote their time and skills to supporting users in the best way possible, often as teachers or partners in research.

And what of the debate over the need for bricks and mortar? To be sure, projects that bring research material online are welcome developments, bringing us one step closer to the ideal of the universal library—as desirable today as it was in the reign of the Ptolemies. But ironically, while the information critical to scholarship and the public good is becoming more accessible than ever in the twenty-first century, access alone is rarely enough to serve the needs of scholarship, teaching, learning, and public inquiry today. The authors of this volume examine many of these needs and show how the library is uniquely suited to meet them. In these essays, the library as place is very much alive.

The perspectives and examples offered here are meant to provoke thinking and discussion among those who are planning new space or are considering the future of their libraries. Library planners may wish to explore more deeply some of the ideas raised by the authors, such as the development of off-site repositories or planning for technology, or to learn more about the planning experiences of other institutions. As a supplement to the references provided within the essays, we have listed additional references on the following pages.

K. S.

For Further Reading

The references that follow are intended to give readers more detailed information on special considerations in library design. We include references to specific libraries so that readers may draw on additional examples of recent work.

Special thanks to Joan Lippincott, of the Coalition for Networked Information, for suggesting sources on technology-enabled learning, and to Scott Bennett, from whose extensive literature review on library planning[1] we selected several titles under General Planning. Please note that these lists are suggestive rather than exhaustive.

General Planning

Brand, Steward. 1994. *How Buildings Learn: What Happens after They're Built*. New York: Viking.

Dowler, L. ed. 1997. *Gateways to Knowledge: The Role of Academic Libraries in Teaching, Learning, and Research*. Cambridge, Mass.: MIT Press.

Hurt, Charlene. 2000. The Johnson Center Library at George Mason University. In T. D. Webb, ed., *Building Libraries for the 21st Century: The Shape of Information*. Jefferson, N.C.: McFarland.

Leighton, Philip D., and David C. Weber. 1999. *Planning Academic and Research Library Buildings*, third ed. Chicago: American Library Association.

Marshall, John Douglas. 2004. *Place of Learning, Place of Dreams: A History of the Seattle Public Library*. Seattle: University of Washington Press.

National Library of Medicine and Association of Academic Health Sciences Libraries. 2004. *The Library as Place: Symposium on Building and Revitalizing Health Sciences Libraries in the Digital Age*, November 5–6, 2003. DVD-ROM. Bethesda, Md.: National Library of Medicine.

Ober, John. 2000. Library Services at California State University Monterey Bay. In T. D. Webb, ed. *Building Libraries for the 21st Century: The Shape of Information*. Jefferson, N.C.: McFarland.

Stoffle, Carla J., and Karen Williams. 1995. The Instructional Program and Responsibilities of the Teaching Library. *New Directions for Higher Education* 90: 63–75.

---

[1] See http://www.clir.org/pubs/reports/pub122/part4.html.

Sutton, Lynn Sorensen. 2000. Imagining Learning Spaces at Wayne State University's New David Adamany Undergraduate Library. *Research Strategies* 17: 139–146.

Welch Medical Library Architectural Study. Available at http://www.welch.jhu.edu/architecturalstudy/index.html.

Shared/Offsite Print Repositories

Bridegam, Willis E. 2001. *A Collaborative Approach to Collection Storage: The Five-College Library Depository*. Washington, D.C.: Council on Library and Information Resources. Available at http://www.clir.org/pubs/abstract/pub97abst.html.

Kohl, David. 2003. Paper and Digital Repositories in the United States. *LIBER Quarterly* 13: 241–253. Available at http://liber.library.uu.nl/publish/articles/000038/article.pdf.

Reilly, Bernard F., Jr., with research and analysis by Barbara DesRosiers. 2003. *Developing Print Repositories: Models for Shared Preservation and Access*. Washington, D.C.: Council on Library and Information Resources. Available at http://www.clir.org/pubs/abstract/pub97abst.html.

Luther, Judy, Linda Bills, Amy McColl, Norm Medeiros, Amy Morrison, Eric Pumroy, and Peggy Seiden. 2003. *Library Buildings and the Building of a Collaborative Research Collection at the Tri-College Library Consortium*. Washington, D.C.: Council on Library and Information Resources. Available at http://www.clir.org/pubs/abstract/pub115abst.html.

Technology and IT-Library Collaboration

Beagle, Donald. 1999. Conceptualizing an Information Commons. Includes commentaries by Martin Halbert and Philip J. Tramdack. *Journal of Academic Librarianship* 25(2): 82-93.

Cowgill, Allison, Joan Beam, and Lindsey Wess. 2001. Implementing an Information Commons in a University Library. *Journal of Academic Librarianship* 27(6): 432–439.

Crockett, Charlotte, Sarah McDaniel, and Melanie Remy. 2002. Integrating Services in the Information Commons. *Library Administration & Management* 16(4): 181–186.

Designing the Space: A Conversation with Willliam J. Mitchell. 2003. *Syllabus* 17(2): 10–13, 41. Available at http://www.campus-technology.com/article.asp?id=8105.

Dewey, Barbara I. 2002. University of Tennessee's Collaborative Digital Media Spaces. *ARL: A Bimonthly Report on Research Library Issues and Activities* 222 (June): 4–5. Available at http://www.arl.org/newsltr/222/index.html.

Duncan, J. 1998. The Information Commons: A Model for 'Physical' Digital Resource Centers. *Bulletin of the MLA* 86(4): 576–582.
Haas, Leslie, and Jan Robertson. 2004. *The Information Commons. SPEC Kit 281.* Washington, D.C.: Association of Research Libraries.

Holmes-Wong, Deborah, Marianne Afifi, Shahla Bahvar, and Xioyang Liu. 1997. If You Build It, They Will Come: Spaces, Values and Services in the Digital Era. *Library Administration and Management* 9(2): 74–85.

Lippincott, Joan K. 2002. Developing Collaborative Relationships: Librarians, Students, and Faculty Creating Learning Communities. *C & RL News* 63(3).

Lippincott, Joan K. 2005 forthcoming. New Library Facilities: Opportunities for Collaboration. *Resource Sharing and Information Networks* 17(1-2).

Lippincott, Joan. K. 2005 forthcoming. Net Generation Students and Libraries. In Diana Oblinger and Jim Oblinger, eds., *Educating the Net Generation.* Boulder, Colo.: EDUCAUSE.

National Learning Infrastructure Initiative. 2004. Leading the Transition from Classrooms to Learning Spaces. An NLII White Paper. Proceedings of 2004 Fall Focus Session, Learning Space Designed for the 21st Century, Sept. 9–10, 2004, Cambridge, Mass. Available at http://www.educause.edu/2004FallFocusSession/2672.

McCloskey, Paul. 2003. Designing New Learning Environments: Students Share Control in Classrooms of the Future. *Syllabus* 17(3): 28–30.

McKinstry, Jill, and Peter McCracken. 2002. Combining Computing and Reference Desks in an Undergraduate Library: A Brilliant Innovation or a Serious Mistake? *Portal: Libraries and the Academy* 2(3): 391–400.

Monahan, Torin. 2002. Flexible Space and Built Pedagogy: Emerging IT Embodiments. *Inventio* 4(1): 1–19. Available at http://www.torin-monahan.com/papers/Inventio.html.

Schoomer, Elia. 2000. Electronic Classrooms and Buildings of the Future. Current Issues Roundtable. EDUCAUSE 2000, Nashville, Tennessee, October 10–13, 2000. Available at http://www.educause.edu/ir/library/pdf/EDU0074.pdf.

Simons, Kevin, James Young, and Craig Gibson. 2000. The Learning Library in Context: Community, Integration, and Influence. *Research Strategies* 17(2-3): 123–132.

Stewart, M. Claire, and H. Frank Cervone. 2003. Building a New Infrastructure for Digital Media: Northwestern University Library. *Information Technology and Libraries* 22(2): 69–74.

TLT Group. Teaching/Learning Activities and Learning Spaces that Make them Easier. Available at http://www.tltgroup.org/programs/Teach/Smart_Classrooms.htm.

Valenti, Mark S. 2002. Creating the Classroom of the Future. EDUCAUSE Review (Sept/Oct): 52–62. Available at http://www.educause.edu/ir/library/pdf/erm0254.pdf.

Wilson, Lizabeth A. 2002. Collaborate or Die: Designing Library Space. *ARL: A Bimonthly Report on Research Library Issues and Activities* 222 (June): 1–2. Available at http://www.arl.org/newsltr/222/index.html.

Selected Web Sites

Collaborative Facilities: http://www.dartmouth.edu/~collab/ *A Joint Project of the Coalition for Networked Information and Dartmouth College, as of June 2004 this site features key planning and supporting documents from the following institutions: Dartmouth College, Dickinson College, Northwestern University, Oregon State University, University of Arizona, University of Oregon, University of Southern Illinois—Carbondale, and University of Tennessee.*

Denison University Learning Spaces Project: http://www.denison.edu/learningspaces/

Emory University InfoCommons: http://infocommons.emory.edu/

Georgia Institute of Technology Library and Information Center: http://www.library.gatech.edu

Indiana University Information Commons: http://www.ic.indiana.edu/

Marquette Center for Teaching and Learning: http://www.marquette.edu/ctl/index.htm

Ohio University Learning Commons: http://www.library.ohiou.edu/libinfo/lc/index.htm

Stanford University Wallenberg Hall: http://wallenberg.stanford.edu/

University of Arizona Integrated Learning Center: http://www.ilc.arizona.edu/

University of Calgary Information Commons: http://www.ucalgary.ca/ic/

University of Chicago Crerar Computing Cluser & CyberCafe: http://intech.uchicago.edu/ccc/clusters/crerar.html

University of Georgia Student Learning Center: http://www.libs.uga.edu/slc/

University of Iowa Information Arcade: http://www.lib.uiowa.edu/arcade/

University of Southern California Leavey Library Information Commons: http://www.usc.edu/isd/libraries/locations/leavey/spaces/#infocommons

University of Toronto Scotiabank Information Commons: http://www.utoronto.ca/welcome.html/

University of Washington University Libraries Media Center: http://www.lib.washington.edu/media/

Vassar College Media Cloisters: http://mediacloisters.vassar.edu

Wellesley College Knapp Media and Technology Center: http://www.wellesley.edu/Knapp/mtc.html